The *Marriage* INSTITUTION

The *Marriage* INSTITUTION

SET UP BY GOD

REVEREND JOYCE NYANTE

XULON PRESS

Xulon Press
2301 Lucien Way #415
Maitland, FL 32751
407.339.4217
www.xulonpress.com

Paperback ISBN-13: 978-1-6628-0925-5

Ebook ISBN-13: 978-1-6628-0926-2

Dedication

I dedicate this book to my late father, W. K. Nimako Mensah, who was an honorable and courageous man whose generosity and good works were a virtue that went beyond his name. I also dedicate this book to my mother, Lucy Nimako Mensah, who is a beautiful and humble *Proverbs 31* woman.

This book is dedicated to my sisters and brothers in the Great Nimako-Mensah family, who challenged me to work hard so I can present myself to God and receive God's approval to be a good worker, one who does not need to be ashamed and who correctly explains the word of truth.

They are:

My late sister, Evangelist Janet Danso, who introduced me to the book of Revelations when I was as young as six years old.

My brother, Alex Nimako Mensah, who is the most patient and kind person I have ever known and who taught me Psalm 133 and said to me, "memorize this and repeat it every morning on your way to school."

My sister, Apostle Christiana Agyei, who never, ever said *no* to me and who has stood as a strong spiritual pillar in the family and for that reason, has attained a special family title, The Spirit Helper.

My sister Minister Cecilia Oteng-Pabi who taught me how to be brave and tough and stand up for myself, while at the same time, she retains a remarkable and very pleasant peacemaking attitude.

My sister, Prophetess Juliana Kyeremateng, who is very calm and easy-going and whose prophecy over my first daughter's life in August 1991 was fulfilled five months afterward. My sister is awesome!

My brother, Pastor Patrick Nimako Mensah. The doctors said he would not live long due to sickle cell illness at age six, but God proved His mighty power and my brother still lives on over forty years later. He operates in a unique anointing of God on his life that enables him to preach the good news of our Lord Jesus Christ in a powerful way.

Finally, my dearest sister Modda Eugenia Nimako Mensah, the last of us all and whose life is nothing less of a miracle.

I dedicate this book to my father-in-law, Colonel E. O. Nyante. He impacted some of the knowledge about different traditions and cultural marriages I will be writing about.

I also dedicate this book to my mother-in-law, Josephine Nyante, who was an industrious woman who feared God and kept His commandments.

I dedicate this book to my husband, Pastor Simeon Nyante, who stands by me for better and for worse and till death do us part.

I also dedicate this book to my daughter Lady Anna and her daughter (my grandbaby) Kennedi Aniya Buckner.

My precious daughter Simone, who rests in the safe and loving arms of the Lord. My daughter Princess Sarah, just finished high school. My daughter Queen Esther in high school. They are most wonderful, blessed, and favored by the Lord. I pray that boundary lines fall for them in pleasant places as they attain a delightful inheritance in God. Also that they shall be taught by the Lord, and great shall be their peace. Amen

Table of Contents

Introduction

My hope is that by reading this book, you will learn to take authority over your marriage and form it as a relationship of endless love and learning. I pray God gives you the spirit of wisdom and revelation in the knowledge of Him. Also, I pray that the eyes of your understanding be enlightened. Through that enlightenment, you may come to know what the hope of God's calling for you is, and what the riches of the glory of God's inheritance are. Furthermore, I want you to know of the exceeding greatness of God's power, according to His wonderous working in Christ, through his death resurrection and ascension. Thus, He resides far above all principality, power, might, and dominion, and every name that is named, not only in this world, but also in that which is to come. Finally, I pray that you will be encouraged by God putting all things under Jesus's feet, and gave Him to be the head over all things to the church, which is His body, and by that He has fulfilled all things concerning you. Amen.

This book can be used by professionals for teaching, counseling, and training. Married couples can use this book to strengthen their marriages. And singles who are preparing to enter marriage can also use this book for guidelines to support them make the right choice. This book is also a knowledge and educative material and can be read by anyone who loves to read books.

My Pre-Marriage Encounter With God

When I was nineteen years old, one of my mentors said to me, "Joyce, start praying for your marriage." That direction took me to another level in my Christian walk and a divine encounter with God.

I prayed that God would reveal my husband to me. I asked God to make my future husband very obvious, so I would know he is the man I am meant to marry when I met him. God answered my prayers. It took about two years for God's revelations to be complete.

The first revelation I saw was a handsome man standing by a blue Peugeot. Then, God showed me that the man owned a business and that he was doing business in several countries. I also heard a voice in another revelation telling me that the man belonged to the Baptist Church. I knew it was God's voice because there was no one near me as I entered my office that day.

After these revelations, I prayed God would bring the man to my church, the Miracle Life Christian Centre. I was incredibly involved in my church within the teaching and evangelistic ministry, and I was not ready to go looking for someone in another church.

At some point in time, my church was going into home-cells outreach and the Lord used me and other saints to open over fifteen cell groups in various homes in different neighborhoods in the first six months of the church being planted.

Well, it happened that my then unknown husband Simeon's brother heard about a new word-based church in the neighborhood opening home cells and asked his father and the rest of their family to come visit this new church who are opening cells everywhere. By that time, Simeon was in Zurich for a business trip. After his return from Zurich, Simeon's siblings had attended my church numerous times and had become comfortable and started membership processing. So they asked him to give them a ride to church one Sunday morning and he brought them. He decided to stay and attend the service. That Sunday, I was on stage with the Senior Pastor preaching when they came in. And as soon as I saw Simeon, God confirmed he was the man I would marry.

Simeon's Pre-Marriage Encounter With God

When Simeon took his brothers to church that day, he saw me on stage but did not like me. He thought, "Who is that skinny lady standing there talking and talking?" After the service, Simeon asked his brothers who I was. Simeon started praying seriously for his marriage after he had become a regular visitor to my church. After praying for a while, he had a revelation that he was sitting at the top of a well and then a dove came out of the well and sat beside him. Suddenly, as he was gazing at the dove, it turned into a lady, and that lady was me. When Simeon woke up, he understood his dream, but he told God, "I cannot marry that hard, skinny, talkative lady who teaches and preaches all over the church and is everyone's sister and friend. I cannot even begin to think of how I would approach her and tell her about my encounter in my dream and therefore, my marriage intentions."

Instead, Simeon went and narrated his dream to a man known within the body of Christ to be a renowned counselor to receive counseling. The man instructed Simeon to pray for boldness. From that point on, Simeon sought out the Lord's help through intensive prayers for boldness and wisdom to approach this whole marriage intention in a manner that he would not mess up.

One day, people stood outside church to take pictures. Simeon asked me to take a picture with him. I, however, said I was allergic to photos and I would not show in the developed picture. Simeon realized his first approach did not go well, so he went on his Plan B.

After a prayer meeting one Friday evening, he came up to me and said he wanted to visit me at home. I agreed and we scheduled the visit. Unfortunately, Simeon did not turn up because he could not gather enough courage. Not knowing Simeon was not going to show up, I prepared light refreshments for my guest. When he did not show up, I packed up the snacks and intended to throw them at him in church the next Sunday morning.

As soon as Simeon saw me at church that Sunday morning, he apologized immediately. So, I let it go, then politely asked him to follow me home for the snack after the service, which he did. The next time we met was in his parent's home. I went to plant a home cell group in their house because his parents had become incredibly involved in the church and offered to host a cell group for bible study. I was the Cells Coordinator for the church at that time.

Simeon was present on the inauguration day of the home cell, but after that, he went to live in a different county. So, he only attended church occasionally when he visited his family.

After a while, Simeon moved back home to his parents' house, where we had the cell group established. I also started seeing him at most meetings. Six weeks later, we were together. Simeon told me about his revelation. I told him mine. We both agreed we were made for each other. So he was fighting what he knew belonged to him all along because he was afraid and also said he was not ready to take up a marriage responsibility. But Simeon could not fight nor fear forever, because God intended to bless and honor me. After six weeks, I was betrothed to Simeon. We got engaged three months later. Then wedding bells rang four months after our engagement. And at the time of this writing, we have been married thirty-one years

Our wedding

One year of marriage

Ten years of marriage

Twenty years of marriage

Thirty years of marriage

Chapter 1

God's Empowerment to Mankind to Dominate and Rule.

God said, Let Us [Father, Son, and Holy Spirit] make mankind in Our image, after Our likeness, and let them have complete authority over the fish of the sea, the birds of the air, the [tame] beasts, and over all of the earth, and over everything that creeps upon the earth. So God created man in His own image, in the image and likeness of God He created him; male and female He created them. God blessed them; and God said to them, "Be fruitful and multiply, and fill the earth, and subdue it; and rule over the fish of the sea and over the birds of the sky and over every living thing that moves on the earth. — Genesis 1:26–28 AMP

God created men and women in His image—His spiritual personality and moral likeness—and gave them complete authority over the earth. Their authority allowed them to rule and subdue, which are natural instincts that manifest the moment a child is born. When two children are put together to play, one child naturally tries to take a toy away from the other child. That leads the other children to fight over the same toy. Then you find that they both want to exercise authority over that one same toy.

Another scenario is when an adult walk in the room to pick up one child, you find that the other child also wants to be picked up at the same time.

This authority to rule and dominate is a God-given ability. When children are old enough to go to school, they begin to exhibit various types of rulership abilities and they naturally branch into various leadership roles and positions. This behavior is reflected in society. Throughout our lives, we rule in different stages and take up responsibilities by exercising this natural tendency to rule, subdue, and dominate. And this drive enables what we become as we advance in life, alongside exhibiting different behavior patterns.

A marriage consists of two rulers, and when two rulers occupy the same territory, there can be friction if wisdom is not exercised.

In God's divine ability to empower people to dominate and rule, he also positioned men as the head and women as helpmates. Genesis 2:18 (NASB) states, "Then the LORD God said, 'It is not good for the man to be alone; I will make him a helper suitable for him.'" And so, each of us rules in our God-ordained positions. The helpmate is not a subordinate to the head and, for that matter, to be oppressed, bullied, or mistreated. Instead, the helpmate must exercise her authority, skills, and rule by standing beside her husband as support.

I personally believe that a helper is the strongest personality, because she must be strong for herself before she can help and support the head. Many societies, homes, and families have fallen apart because the female authority to rule and dominate as a helpmate was not acknowledged or permitted to function.

Chapter 2

What Is Marriage?

*M*arriage is an intimate, personal union between a man and a woman, which is consummated and continuously nourished through sexual intercourse. It is perfected through a lifelong partnership of mutual love and commitment.

Marriage is also a social institution regulated by God's Word through the laws and customs that society develops to safeguard its continuity and welfare.

God created man and woman for each other. Their essential natures are complementarily, meant to create oneness in marriage.

Here are some biblical references on how God intended and how He instituted marriage from the beginning of creation:

Genesis 2:24 (NASB) states, "For this reason a man shall leave his father and his mother and be joined to his wife; and they shall become one flesh."

Matthew 19:4–6 (NASB) states, "And He answered and said, 'Have you not read that He who created them from the beginning made them male and female," and said, 'for this reason a man shall leave his father and mother and be joined to his wife, and the two shall become one flesh. So they are no longer two, but one flesh. What therefore God has joined together let no man separate.'"

Ephesians 5:31 (NASB) states, "For this reason a man shall leave his father and mother and shall be joined to his wife, and the two shall become one flesh."

Marriage is a ministry that is developed with time. Therefore, in this school of ministry, learning does not end until spouses are separated by death. We are all subject to changes in emotions, physical appearance, finances, jobs, communication, views, dreams, beliefs, and more. So then, only time tells how we excel into perfection in this school of ministry, which is attended day by day, hour by hour, and minute by minute. We must stay abreast with changes in our surroundings, social cycles, economy, experiences, and encounters with one another, ensuring a positive reflection or impact on this school. Basically, we need to exercise our God-given wisdom in our authority to rule, subdue, and dominate in this school, so it is just how God-ordained and designed it to be. Hence, let us look at wisdom and types and how they relate to this marriage school ministry.

Wisdom

+ Natural wisdom is the application of facts and knowledge that we derive from our studies and life experiences. Natural wisdom may not always work in marriage, so if it is your sole source of wisdom, your marriage may experience instability.

+ Fallen supernatural wisdom is a corrupted moral and spiritual wisdom contrary to the wisdom of God. It is the result of sin. James 3:15 (KJV) states, "This wisdom descendeth not from above, but is earthly, sensual and devilish." Fallen supernatural wisdom opposes every good thing God has instore for marriage, so if it is exercised in marriage, the marriage is bound to fail.

+ Biblical wisdom is the application of God's Word in our lives. God wants us to use biblical wisdom in our marriages. John 15:7 (KJV) states, "If ye abide in me and my word abide in you, ye shall ask what ye will, and it shall be done unto you." God knows how to make two people with different backgrounds and interests become parallel and make wonderful marriage partners.

Marriage is not a human-devised plan to create a convenient way to sort out social responsibilities. If marriage were a human invention, different types of marriage could have equal value. Polygamy—the taking of several wives—may serve an agricultural society better than an industrialized society. Polyandry—the sharing of a wife by several husbands—may prove to be more efficient and economical in a technologically advanced society. Monogamy—the lifelong union of one man to one woman—would have no more intrinsic value than any other type of marriage. Some could argue that monogamy has served its purpose as the ideal norm of society and should now be replaced by serial monogamy, the taking of a succession of husbands and wives. In fact, for many today, the latter better satisfies the quest for greater self-fulfillment and gratification.

The Bible presents marriage as a divine institution. If marriage were of human origin, then we would have the right to decide the kind of marital relationship each of us want. Marriage, however, began with God when he created the world.

As the creator of marriage, God has the right to tell us which principles should govern our marital relationships.

If God had left us no instructions about marriage after establishing it, then marriage could be regulated according to personal rudiments. But He did not leave us in the dark. Within the Bible, God reveals His will for the nature and function of marriage. When we choose to live according to God's will, we have to respect biblical principles that govern marriage, divorce, and remarriage. Some state laws ignore, or violate, God's teachings in the Bible. In such cases, we must obey God rather than any human authority, as the Bible says in the book of Acts, the fifth chapter and verse number twenty-nine.

Chapter 3

Before Marriage

*G*enesis 2:24 (NASB) states, "For this reason a man shall leave his father and his mother and be joined to his wife; and they shall become one flesh." Hebrews 13:4 states, "Marriage is to be held in honor among all, and the marriage bed is to be undefiled; for fornicators and adulterers God will judge." This is translated to mean that couples should not live together before marriage. God does not recommend living together before marriage because it is a creation of human thinking and a man-made arrangement.

In my numerous years of counseling couples, I find there are more problems in such association of living together as though people are a couple but are actually not. This is simply because mankind is trying to put in place something which is out of place, therefore, it attracts everything outside the perfect *will* of God for mankind, consequently, no blessing from God at all on that union. Fornication is the most common sin that comes with living together before an actual marriage. This choice can also lead to arguments about money, family disapproval, and more. Misunderstandings may lead to physical and verbal abuse. Some couples can grow to hate each other and become enemies. They may split up after intertwining their finances. Concerning couples who move in and live together before marriage, when they do finally get married, you find that most of such marriages may not last because they did not start right.

In the scenarios described above, both people waiver and have divided loyalty between God and themselves and therefore are unstable in everything they do. This occurs because they are seriously using every effort to please and satisfy one another; anxiety becomes inevitable whereas they hesitate to offend each other. They are unsettled as a wave of the sea that is blown and tossed by the wind. And such people should not expect to receive anything from the Lord whiles in that state of violating God's divine principle of marriage.

Some people recommend that the only way to truly know someone before getting married is to live together and see if the relationship will work out. God, however, wants us to put our trust in Him for all things. He has a plan for us. Jeremiah 29:11-13 (NASB) states, "'For I know the plans that I have for you,' declares the LORD, 'plans for welfare and not for calamity to give you a future and a hope. Then you will call upon Me and come and pray to Me, and I will listen to you. You will seek Me and find Me when you search for Me with all your heart.'"

The book of first Corinthians , second chapter, ninth verse says, "eye hath not seen, nor ear heard, neither have entered into the heart of man, the things which God hath prepared for them that love him."

Furthermore, the book of first Peter, the fifth chapter and the eleventh verse say, "all power belongs to God now and forever. Hence, we do not need to be carried away by fear to think that people must move in together to try out partners before they find the right one. For if we serve God, then let us also trust Him and believe that He will see us through all live stages."

In the Bible, book of Matthew chapter five, verses twenty-seven and twenty-eight, Jesus said, in His sermon on the mount, that, "You have heard that it was said, 'You shall not commit adultery. I, however, say that everyone who looks at another person with lust has already com- mitted adultery." So you might say you and your partner are strong enough to live together without sinning against God. Jesus, however, believes you do not have to physi- cally commit sin in order to commit adultery, just a lustful look is enough. There are consequences. Therefore, if we choose to operate in a fallen supernatural wisdom which is a corrupted moral and spiritual wisdom—contrary to the wisdom of God—you reap negative consequences.

However, if we choose biblical wisdom, we reap God's blessings in our marriages as well as every area of our lives. These extended blessings apply to generations after us. The word of God in Exodus 20:6 (KJV) states, "And showing mercy unto thousands of generations that love me and keep my commandments."

Chapter 4

The Bible's View on Homosexuality and Sexual Immorality

*T*his topic was not originally planned to be incorporated in this test book, but I felt God's calling to include it since it has become a major topic of conversation relating to marriage. Some educational institutions are even making the teaching and study of homosexuality an inclusion in their curriculum in recent years. Hence, I would like to explain the words, *homosexuality* and *sexual immorality* before I proceed.

- Homosexuality is described as a person who is sexually attracted to people of their own sex.
- Sexual immorality is the evil ascribed to sexual acts that violate social conventions.
- Immorality is iniquity, wickedness, and morally objectionable behavior.

Now, in order to proceed on the subject, I would like to first refer to certain scriptures of the Bible.

1. See to it that no one takes you captive through philosophy and empty deception, according to the tradition of men, according to the elementary principles of the world, rather than according to Christ, Colossians 2:8 (NASB).

2. For since the creation of the world His invisible attributes, His eternal power and divine nature, have been clearly seen, being understood through what has been made, so that they are without excuse. For even though they knew God, they did not honor Him as God or give thanks, but they became futile in their speculations, and their foolish heart was darkened. Professing to be wise, they became fools, and exchanged the glory of the incorruptible God for an image in the form of corruptible man and of birds and four-footed animals and crawling creatures. Therefore God gave them over in the lusts of their hearts to impurity, so that their bodies would be dishonored among them. For they exchanged the truth of God for a lie and worshiped and served the creature rather than the Creator, who is blessed forever. Amen. For this reason God gave them over to degrading passions; for their women exchanged the natural function for that which is unnatural, and in the same way also the men abandoned the natural function of the woman and burned in their desire toward one another, men with men committing indecent acts and receiving in their own persons

the due penalty of their error. And just as they did not see fit to acknowledge God any longer, God gave them over to a depraved mind, to do those things which are not proper, being filled with all unrighteousness, wickedness, greed, evil; full of envy, murder, strife, deceit, malice; they are gossips, slanderers, haters of God, insolent, arrogant, boastful, inventors of evil, disobedient to parents, without understanding, untrustworthy, unloving, unmerciful; and although they know the ordinance of God, that those who practice such things are worthy of death, they not only do the same, but also give hearty approval to those who practice them, Romans 1:20–32 (NASB).

3. Or do you not know that the unrighteous will not inherit the kingdom of God? Do not be deceived; neither fornicators, nor idolaters, nor adulterers, nor effeminate, nor homosexuals, nor thieves, nor the covetous, nor drunkards, nor revilers, nor swindlers, will inherit the kingdom of God. Such were some of you; but you were washed, but you were sanctified, but you were justified in the name of the Lord Jesus Christ and in the Spirit of our God, 1 Corinthians 6:9–11 (NASB).

4. We know that the law is good if one uses it properly. We also know that the law is made not for the righteous but for lawbreakers and rebels, the ungodly and sinful, the unholy and irreligious, for those who kill their fathers or mothers, for

murderers, for the sexually immoral, for those practicing homosexuality, for slave traders and liars and perjurers—and for whatever else is contrary to the sound doctrine that conforms to the gospel concerning the glory of the blessed God, which he entrusted to me, 1 Timothy 1:8–11 (NASB).

The Bible references above mentions homosexuality and all iniquity being contrary to the sound doctrine of God. For that matter, we know beyond any doubt that homosexuality and sex changes are not of God. The world laws may change to incorporate homosexuality and all such like but the truth of the matter is it does not make it right. "All things are lawful for me, but not all things are profitable. All things are lawful for me, but all things edify not," first Corinthians, chapter ten, verse twenty-three. It explains how mankind has the right to do whatever they please and it can be even lawful, meaning the laws of the land can even favor you to do something. But it may not be profitable nor edifying to you, to surroundings and to society. So then, one must consider certain factors before doing anything, especially before considering homosexuality, such as, *How benefiting is the act? How healthy is the act? How valuable is the act? How acceptable is the act?* and other similar criteria. Further scripture in Proverbs, chapter fourteen, verse twelve, says there is a way that seems right unto a man, but the end thereof are the ways of death. So we find that an act which might be lawful or acceptable may not necessarily be expedient or healthy and might even lead to death. So let us not be weary in always running back to God to help us any time we find that something in our lives is not going in accordance with divine principle.

Homosexuality is a destructive force to society and even to surrounding people in communities. It has been realized that those who come out to declare to society that they are homosexuals, usually have battled with it for a while. And then the declaration is more or less like a war on society, literally saying, "I'm gay, what are you gonna do?"

If homosexuality was part of God's creation, people would not have to fight for their sexuality to be accepted, but rather, it would be embraced graciously. Why should it be announced? Why should it cause shock and surprise among families and friends? First Thessalonians, chapter four, verse three says, "this is the will of God, your sanctification; that is, that you abstain from sexual immorality." This means, in our process of acquiring sanctity—being made or becoming holy—we should avoid the evil ascribed to sexual acts.

You see King David said in Psalms, book one-hundred verse thirty-nine, that God formed our inward parts and wove man in his mother's womb, so man is fearfully and wonderfully made and this wonder is beyond human imagination. He goes on to say that the souls of men know this very well due to the nature of God in man. So God made us with no mistakes whatsoever and every living being knows it. Humanity is designed to be either male or female, with complementary sexual equipment.

We are intended to grow through childhood and enter puberty, then be attracted to the opposite sex. God created man in His own image, male and female He created us. We know that God blessed us and said to us to be fruitful and multiply, and fill the earth, and subdue it; and rule over the fish of the sea and over the birds of the sky and over every living thing that moves on the earth. But I guess some people have intentionally developed their abilities and authority in a paradigm shift from how God created male and female and this has hardened their hearts. This is the problem that the Bible addresses in the first book of Corinthians, chapter one and verses eighteen to twenty-five, which talks about how the word of the cross is foolishness to those who are perishing—meaning those in a paradigm shift. But to us who are being saved, meaning those who agree, accept, and adhere to the Word of God, it represents the power of God. The verses continue to say that God will destroy the wisdom of the wise, and the cleverness of the clever will be set aside.

Where is the wise man or philosopher? Where is the scholar? Where is the debater or logician of this age? Has God not exposed the foolishness of this world's wisdom? For, since in the wisdom of God, the world through its wisdom did not come to know God. God was well-pleased through the simplicity of the preaching the story of the death of Jesus on the cross to save those who believe. For indeed Jews ask for signs and Greeks search for wisdom; but we preach Christ crucified, to Jews a stumbling block and to Gentiles foolishness, but to those who are the called, both Jews, Greeks or Gentiles, Christ Jesus is the power of God and the wisdom of God. Because the foolishness of God is wiser than men, and the weakness of God is stronger than men. Hallelujah!

For some, the significance of the cross on which Jesus died is offensive because they do not believe they are sinful and in need of rescuing. For others, the cross is foolishness because it addresses a spiritual world they do not consider to be important to the life they lead. This is by no means a problem limited to homosexuals. The Bible spoke about humanity in general, as we are all sinful in one way or another.

These immoralities happened in Sodom and Gomorrah, which is why God sent angels to warn Lot. But when the men in the land of Sodom and Gomorrah heard that two men had come to visit with Lot, they demanded that Lot give them the angels that God sent, so they could sleep with them. Lot pleaded with the men in the land and told them to take his virgin daughters instead of the angels. But the men in the land however, wanted the angels who were visiting Lot.

The men in the land wanted the angels so bad that while Lot was preventing them, they started to argue with him, saying to Lot how he was an alien in the land but had come to make himself a judge over them. The men of the land went on to say to Lot, "Now we will treat you worse than them if you do not allow us to have them." So, they pressed hard against Lot and came near to break his door. But the angels who were inside Lot's house reached out their hands and brought Lot into the house with them and shut the door.

The angels struck the men who were at the doorway of the house with blindness, both small and great, so that they wearied themselves trying to find the doorway. Then the two angels said to Lot, "Whom else have you here? A son-in-law, and your sons, and your daughters, and whomever you have in the city, bring them out of the place; for we are about to destroy this place, because their outcry has become so great before the LORD that the LORD has sent us to destroy it."

Lot went out and spoke to his sons-in-law, who were to marry his daughters, and said, "Up, get out of this place, for the LORD will destroy the city." When morning dawned, the angels urged Lot, saying, "Up, take your wife and your two daughters who are here, or you will be swept away in the punishment of the city." But Lot hesitated. So, the angels seized his hand and the hand of his wife and the hands of his two daughters, for the compassion of the LORD was upon Lot; and the angels brought them out and put them outside the city. When they had brought them outside, the angels said to Lot and his household, "Escape for your life! Do not look behind you, and do not stay anywhere in the valley; escape to the mountains, or you will be swept away." So the LORD rained on Sodom and Gomorrah brimstone and fire from the LORD out of heaven, and He overthrew those cities, and all the valley, and all the inhabitants of the cities, and what grew on the ground because of their immoral and inhuman acts and He saved only Lot and his family. The reference is from Genesis, the nineteenth chapter and the first twenty-five verses.

These kinds of immoralities which happened in Sodom and Gomorrah, immoralities that led God to destroy whole nations with mighty people are what is happening today—same sex relationships and same sex marriages. This is mankind's decision. It is not of God at all and it is not right. God did not make mistakes when He created human beings. If He wanted to create same-sex marriage, He would have created beings to engage in same-sex relationships and it would have been perfect and it would have been from the beginning of creation.

Unfortunately, some churches have not proven to be genuine representatives of Christ and have supported, encouraged, promoted the practice of same-sex relationships and same-sex marriages in the church. So people who are sincerely looking to find help, answers, support and deliverance in the church are rather given the okay to carry on practicing and living in same-sex relationships and same sex marriages. They are told most of the time also that God made them that way and so they can serve God just as they are.

But the good news is that there is hope for mankind as long as there is life and a willingness to change. When we look at the Word of God and into the book of Romans 12:1–2 (NASB), the Bible says, "Therefore I urge you, brethren, by the mercies of God, to present your bodies a living and holy sacrifice, acceptable to God, which is your spiritual service of worship. And do not be conformed to this world, but be transformed by the renewing of your mind, so that you may prove what the will of God is, that which is good and acceptable and perfect."

This scripture encourages us to exercise the power of the tongue by speaking the word of God into your life. Affirm you are who God created you to be, and you will remain what God created you to be. Refuse whatever is different from who God says you are. Renounce what your mind or society tells you in contrast with what God says you are. Reject what the devil offers you no matter how attractive, convincing, or promising it may look. Repent and surrender your life to God. Know that God so loved the world, that He gave His only begotten Son, that whoever believes in Him shall not perish, but have eternal life, to the effect that if you were the only human being on earth, Christ would still have come to die for you. For God did not send the Son into the world to judge the world, but that the world might be saved through Him.

Also, renew your mind. How do you do this? Look out for your mental blockers, which are those thoughts, mindsets, ideas, and anything in your mind which blocks you from progressing to newness. Deliberately remove these blockers from your mind and replace them with mental success, which are thoughts that enable progress to newness and refreshing. Tell yourself you are a new person, *you are brand new*. The old you is gone and the new you has come and you will never be the same again. Now all these strength, grace, boldness, and ability to renounce the bad and negative and to tell and affirm the positive to yourself are from God, who reconciled us to Himself through Jesus Christ and gave us the ministry of reconciliation. And so, turn from your sins and wicked ways and God will hear your cry and restore you to where you ought to be by reconciling you back to himself by granting you the enablement.

Chapter 5

Marriage Traditions and Ceremonies from Around the World

*A*s part of the study of this divine institution of marriage which is designed by God, it is important to look at some marriage traditions and cultures from around the world. The diversities and beauties of them all may help explain how a man and woman, from completely different traditions and cultures, can be joined together in holy and peaceful matrimony. Tying the knot in any culture comes with a laundry list of traditions and rituals. Here are some wedding traditions that extend beyond a white dress and a veil.

Chinese Wedding Traditions

On the morning of the wedding, the groom fetches the bride in an elaborate ceremony that often involves tasks—things the groom must do—which are given by the bride's family before they will let the bride be joined with her groom.

There is a pre-wedding tea ceremony hosted by the groom's family. The ceremony is an integral part of any Chinese wedding. It is the formal introduction of the bride to her new in-laws.

Red is the central color in Chinese culture. It is used on the invitations, throughout the decorations, and elsewhere.

The bride and groom have to keep their shoes on from the time they put them on in the morning until the end of the wedding.

It is only after the wedding reception is over that the bride and groom are considered married in the eyes of their friends and families.

Traditionally, the bride returns home as a guest three days after the wedding, bearing gifts for her family. Now, a simple outfit change after the tea ceremony at the groom's home represents the passing of three days.

In modern China, brides pick three wedding dresses. The first dress is a traditional *qipao* or *cheongsam*. This dress is embroidered and slim-fitting, and it is typically red because it is a strong, lucky color in Chinese culture. For the second dress, the bride might choose a white, full-skirt ball gown—a nod to the popularity of Western wedding dress trends. For the third dress, the bride will duck out of the reception to change into a gown or cocktail dress in any color the bride chooses.

French-Canadian Wedding Traditions

The groom and his party meet the bride and her family at the bride's house. They take a procession of cars to the wedding, often honking and yelling to announce their happiness. Anyone they see along the way will shout well-wishes.

The entire wedding party enters the church together.

French women wear white on their wedding days. Some believe the tradition of a white wedding dress originated in France.

The sock dance is an important part of a French-Canadian wedding reception. Unmarried siblings of the bride or the groom wear funny socks and do a silly dance. Guests throw money at the dancers, which the bride and groom later collect.

Some couples play traditional French-Canadian folk music at their receptions as a way to highlight their French roots.

French-Canadians have a sneaky way of avoiding lame wedding gifts. If the invitation says "Presentation only" on the invites, the couple is asking guests to bring money for them instead of traditional wedding gifts.

African-American Wedding Traditions

Broom jumping is most often seen at African-American weddings these days. The tradition is rooted in slavery days, when a marriage between enslaved men and women was not legally recognized. In the antebellum period, enslaved men and women declared their unions by jumping over a broom together and it also symbolizes the start of their new home.

Jewish Wedding Traditions

Sometimes the bride and groom will both wear white on the wedding day to symbolize purity.

Both the bride and groom are walked down the aisle by their respective parents. The parents of the groom escort parents escort him to the *Chuppah*, then the bride and her parents follow.

Jewish brides and grooms traditionally signed an Aramaic document called a *Ketubah* that indicated the bride's acceptance of the groom's proposal and his ownership of her. Modern couples are reviving this tradition, though now it just includes vows of commitment and their love.

Jewish couples say their vows under a *Chuppah*, or wedding canopy, sometimes covered in flowers. It symbolizes the couple's new home.

Breaking a glass is a Jewish wedding tradition. After the ceremony, the groom steps on a cloth-covered glass. This has many meanings, such as the destruction of the Temple in Jerusalem, and a reminder of the fragility of life and sanctity of marriage.

The reception meal begins with *Hamotzi*, a sweet, braided loaf of bread, which is the blessing of the *Challah*.

The *Hora*, or chair dance, is a fun part of Jewish wedding receptions. Brave guests hoist the bride and groom above their heads. They sit on chairs, as guests dance to the sounds of *Hava Nagila* in a circle around them.

Indian Wedding Traditions

In separate, pre-wedding ceremonies, called *mandap muhurat*, both bride and groom are smeared with turmeric, a yellow powder that makes the skin smooth.

Bridal *mehndi*, elaborate henna hand paintings, are an important part of an Indian bride's beauty regimen. Female friends help apply them during a *mehndi* party prior to the wedding.

Red symbolizes good luck in the Indian culture. So, brides wear traditional saris in red or red and white with gold detailing.

The most important part of a Hindu wedding ceremony is *Saptapadi*, or the vow exchange. The bride and groom do so while circling a sacred fire three times. After the first round of exactly seven steps the bride and groom say their vows. After the third round, the groom gives the bride a silver ring as a gesture of love. The couple also exchange flower garlands as additional symbols of love.

Guests at Indian weddings don bright colors, in traditional garb, if possible.

Instead of cake, Indian newlyweds feed each other five bites of a sweet food—usually honey and yogurt.

Spanish Wedding Traditions

It is custom for the groom to give the bride's father a watch after the bride accepts the wedding proposal. The groom also gives the bride thirteen gold coins (*las arras*) as a gift because it symbolizes God's love.

In the past, Spanish women wore black silk dresses, with black lace veils, for their wedding. Now, white dresses are common, and veils are almost always present because they symbolize God's protection.

In the past, men often wore embroidered shirts on their wedding days, handmade by their future wives. Some still adhere to this practice.

Orange blossoms, or *azahares*, are the chosen flower for Spanish weddings. They represent happiness and fulfillment.

Some Spanish couples place their wedding rings on their right hands, not the left.

Spanish wedding receptions are lively, often with a mariachi band. The *Sequidillas Manchegas* is a popular dance performance, too.

Paella, a Spanish stew that contains seafood and rice, is served as part of the meal. Sangria, a boozy cocktail made with wine and fresh fruit, is also traditionally served at weddings.

Japanese Wedding Traditions

Shinto shrines are traditional settings for Japanese weddings. Only the bride and groom's family attends. However, many Western couples do not practice this.

The sharing of sake, or *san san kudo*, is the most important Japanese wedding tradition. The groom, then the bride, takes three sips of rice wine from three different cups. Then the couple offers the *san san kudo* to their families to symbolize a new bond.

Traditionally, brides wear colorful kimonos or *shiromukus*, which are formal Japanese-style gowns. Now, it is standard for brides to wear white, a symbol of purity, then change into an *irouchiakake*, which is a red, gold, silver, and white kimono.

Lobster is common at Japanese wedding receptions because the shell is bright red—the color of luck. Whole clams are also served because they symbolize a couple's unity.

Food is not served in four courses at weddings. Four is an unlucky number for the Japanese. Their word for it is *shi*, and it sounds like their word for death.

Money, *Oshugi*, is the standard wedding gift for a Japanese couple. It is often presented in decorative envelopes called *Shugi-Bukuro*.

Italian Wedding Traditions

In Italy, the land of love, gold wedding rings first became popular. Italy also started the tradition of the wedding cake in the first century B.C. Cake or bread was broken over the bride's head to promote fertility. Sunday is considered the luckiest day for weddings. Some couples tie a knot in front of wedding guests to symbolize their unity. Brides traditionally wear veils to conceal their faces and ward off evil spirits. Guests perform the *Tarantella*, a fast, energetic dance wishing the couple a long, happy future. Guests form a circle and dance around the newlyweds.

Food is paramount at receptions. Some weddings feature as many as fourteen food and drink courses. The courses start with antipasto and end with espresso and cake.

Wine and *grappa* are the chosen drinks at Italian weddings.

The *Evviva gli sposi*, or hurray for the newlyweds, is a common Italian wedding toast. Guests always cheer in response.

Italians often break a glass at the end of the wedding reception. The number of shards of glass symbolizes the number of happy years the couple will have together.

Lebanese Style Weddings

Lebanese-style weddings start with music, dancing, and joyful shouting right outside the groom's doors. This is the *zaffe*, a rowdy, traditional escort made up of friends, family, and sometimes professional musicians and dancers. This group escorts the groom to his bride's house, and then sends them off in a shower of shouted blessings and flower petals.

Greek Wedding Traditions

The bride and groom perform many ceremonial wedding rituals three times to represent the Holy Trinity.

In the past, Greek brides wore yellow or red veils because they represented fire and were said to ward off evil spirits.

Some contemporary brides still mix herbs into their wedding bouquets. Carrying the aromatic plants represents fertility.

Greek wedding receptions sometimes turn into cooking competitions. Guests bring cakes and sweets, or submit recipes, to earn praise.

The *Kalamatiano* is an energetic circle dance the bridal party performs at the reception.

Sometimes, the bride and groom will perform a money dance and guests throw money at them.

At the reception, people smash dishes on the floor for good luck.

Grooms cut up their ties at the end of the wedding reception. The couple then sells the pieces to guests.

Russian Wedding Traditions

Russian grooms have to work for their brides. Before the wedding, the groom shows up at the bride's home and asks for his beloved. In jest, her friends and family refuse him until he brings gifts, money, jewelry, or just his humiliation. Grooms are forced to do silly dances, answer riddles, and perform tests of worthiness like diapering a baby doll. Once the groom impresses friends and family with this bridal ransom, or *vykup nevesty*, he's allowed to meet his bride-to-be.

Peruvian Wedding Traditions

Female guests who are single take part in a tradition a little sweeter than a bouquet toss. Charms attached to ribbons are tucked between the layers of the wedding cake. Before the cake is cut, each woman grabs a ribbon and pulls. At the end of one ribbon is a fake wedding ring. The guest who picks that ribbon is said to be next in line for marriage.

Pakistan Wedding Traditions

After a Pakistani wedding, the couple returns home for a ceremony known as *showing of the face*. Family and friends hold a green shawl over the couple's heads and a mirror as the bride removes the veil she has worn throughout the wedding ceremony. While the newlyweds are busy gazing at one another, the bride's female relatives make off with the groom's shoes and demand money for their safe return.

South Africa Wedding Traditions

Traditional Zulu weddings are marked by vibrant colors and dance-offs between the bride and groom's families. Like many brides across the world, Zulu brides might start the day in a white wedding dress but change into traditional tribal clothing after a church wedding. In a traditional ceremony, the groom's family slaughters a cow to welcome the bride. The bride places money inside the stomach of the cow to symbolize that she is now part of the family.

African Wedding Traditions

Traditions vary from country to country but there are some commonly practiced traditions reflected in most of the African countries' traditions. The common practice of the procedure of an African family agreeing to give their daughter to a man in a marriage union is very similar to the 'Abraham sending his servant to go find a wife for his son, Isaac' scenario in the book of Genesis, the twenty-fourth chapter. In the chapter, Abraham sent his servant, and then the servant took gifts, ten camels from the camels of his master Abraham, and set out with a variety of good things of his master's in his hand. He went to Mesopotamia, to the city of Nahor to find a wife for his master Abraham's son, Isaac.

The servant prayed and asked God to fulfill his mission and God answered his prayers. He found a wife called Rebekah and brought her to Isaac. Now, Abraham's servant realized that God had answered all his prayers because initially, when his master Abraham gave him the task, he prayed to God specifically that God should let the right wife for his master's son Isaac, be the one to give him water to drink and also water his camels. The story continues that before the servant had finished this specific prayer in his heart Rebekah came out with her water jar on her shoulder and she went down to the spring and drew water. And the servant asked her for a drink. She gave him a drink and watered his camels. The servant went on to ask her whose daughter she was and she said she was the daughter of Bethuel, Nahor's son. And this is the family that the servant's master, Abraham, had made him swear to go find a wife from for his son Isaac.

So straight away, the servant put a ring in Rebekah's nose and bracelets on her arms and the servant bowed down and worshipped the Lord and blessed the Lord of his master Abraham who has led him in the right way to find a wife for his master's son Isaac.

When the servant and Rebekah went to her father Bethuel and brother Laban and told them his mission and what had happened as to how he was sent by his master Abraham to come and find a wife for his son from within family. He told them how he had prayed and asked God for specific answers and how all the answers manifested. Hence, he has concluded that Rebekah is the one for his master's son Isaac, and as such, he had come to ask for her hand in marriage for his master's son Isaac. Bethuel and Laban both agreed and permitted Abraham's servant to take Rebekah to be the wife of Isaac.

When Abraham's servant heard their words, he bowed himself to the ground before the Lord and then brought out articles of silver and articles of gold, and garments, and gave them to Rebekah. He also gave precious things to her brother and to her mother. Then he and the men who were with him ate and drank and spent the night. When they arose in the morning, the servant said to Bethuel and Laban to send him away to his master. But her brother and her mother asked that Rebekah stay with them a few days, say ten, and then she may go afterward, but Abraham's servant did not want to be delayed since the Lord had prospered his way, he said. So they called Rebekah and consulted her wishes, asking if she will go with the servant and she said *she will go.* So they sent away their sister, Rebekah, and her nurse with Abraham's servant and his men. They blessed Rebekah and said to her, "May you, our sister, Become thousands of ten-thousands, And may your descendants possess the gate of those who hate them."

So the servant took Rebekah and departed.

Isaac Marries Rebekah—Now Isaac had come from going to Beer-lahai-roi; for he was living in the Negev. He went out to meditate in the field toward evening; and he lifted up his eyes and looked, and behold, camels were coming. Rebekah lifted her eyes, and when she saw Isaac, she dismounted from the camel and said to Abraham's servant, "Who is that man walking in the field to meet us?" And the servant said, "He is my master." Then Rebekah took her veil and covered herself. Abraham's servant told Isaac all the things that he had done. Then Isaac brought Rebekah into his mother, Sarah's, tent, and he took Rebekah, and she became his wife, and he loved her; thus Isaac was comforted because by this time also Isaac's mother Sarah was dead.

Now I would like to walk through the procedure of most African traditional marriages, which is very similar to the process of how Abraham's servant found a wife for his son, Isaac. I am covering this process in about four stages.

In the first stage, after a man finds a woman and both want to get married, the man informs his family members. Those family members then approach the woman's family to present the news. This first stage is referred to as: knocking of door or *betroth*. There is not a serious- commitment at this stage. It just promises marriage to each other and the whole plan can be aborted at any time if things do not go according to plan. This is like the story of the betrothal of Joseph and Mary, the parents of Jesus, and then the birth of Jesus, told in the biblical book of Matthew, chapter one, verses eighteen to nineteen.

This is how it happened. When Jesus's mother Mary had been betrothed to Joseph, before they came together, she was found to be with child by the Holy Spirit. And Joseph her husband, being a righteous man and not wanting to disgrace Mary, planned to send her away secretly.

The second stage takes place after a while or depending on the pace the couple chooses. In this stage, the man's family will visit the woman's family again and set a date for the wedding. The groom's family is provided with a list of items that are acceptable to bring for the bride's hand in marriage. The items are traditionally gifts for the bride, her parents, and a ring for the bride.

The third stage is the day of the wedding ceremony. The two families sit together with lots of friends and loved ones to celebrate. The bride's family is represented by a spokesperson who will, among other things, request the groom's gifts to be inspected by appointees of the bride's family. If all is in accordance, the gifts are accepted, and the bride is officially handed to the groom by her father. The father pronounces his daughter's marriage to the groom and the groom places the ring on her finger and if there is a minister of the gospel present, the two people are blessed by the minister and the minister also will pronounce the two as one. If there is no minister, the father of the bride's pronunciation of the marriage is enough for the marriage to be lawful and binding. This is in accordance with what the Bible said in the book of Genesis, chapter two, verse twenty-four. This reference tells of the reason of marriage and how a man shall leave his father and his mother and be joined to his wife and they shall become one flesh.

During the fourth stage, the married couple returns home together to live under one roof. They are to be fruitful and multiply, according to Genesis the first chapter and the twenty-seventh and twenty-eighth verses. This is where God created man in his own image, in the image of God He created him, and went on to say that He created them male and female. And God blessed them, and God said unto them, be fruitful, and multiply, and replenish the earth, and subdue it and have dominion over the fish of the sea, and over the fowl of the air, and over every living thing that moves upon the earth.

During the wedding ceremony, the couple is free to wear what they like. Most wear white clothes or at least nice clothing.

In some African tribes, however, the bride and groom are tied together at the wrist to symbolize their marriage.

Kola nuts are also essential in some African tribes' medicine and weddings. So, newly married couples share a kola nut with their parents to symbolize the newlyweds' willingness to always help heal each other.

In a *Yoruba* ritual referred to as Tasting the Four Elements, the newlywed couple tastes four flavors that represent a relationship's ups and downs. These flavors include sour, bitter, hot, and sweet. This tradition showcases the couple's willingness to get through the tough times in their marriage and appreciate the sweet. Also, cowrie shells in white, black, and brown colors from West Africa representing fertility and prosperity for them, are commonly used in wedding decorations and cake designs.

Some couples incorporate traditional African clothing. Some go all out, while other weddings favor Western clothing with African elements, including cummerbunds or shawls. Others forgo traditional garb.

European Wedding Traditions

Wedding traditions in Western Europe are as varied as the countries that make up the region. These wonderful, colorful wedding traditions of Western European span almost a quarter of our world.

The engagement ring is still a popular tradition today. It dates back to 860 A.D. when Pope Nicholas I proclaimed that not only was an engagement ring required to seal the agreement to be married, but that the engagement ring must be made in gold. A gold ring signified that the groom was willing to make a financial sacrifice for his bride.

Adding a diamond to the engagement ring took place 617 years later. In the year 1477, King Maximilian presented Mary of Burgundy with a diamond engagement ring.

Medieval Germany started the tradition of having a best man. In those days, it was sometimes necessary for a man to kidnap his bride from a neighboring village and he needed his strongest friend—best man—to help with the kidnapping and to stand by him at the wedding ceremony to fight off any relatives that might try to take her back.

The rhyme "Something old, something new, something borrowed, something blue" refers to the things a bride is supposed to wear on her wedding day to have a successful marriage. And like most superstitions, it does not entirely make sense. There are, of course, many psychology-backed and scientifically grounded ways to have a better marriage. But wearing those four items is a tradition that many people like to keep.

England created many of the wedding traditions we still see today. The ancient nursery rhyme about something old, something new, something borrowed, something blue is now one of the most utilized traditions even though many brides do not know the significance of the rhyme. Something old is symbolic of continuity. The old item was a piece of lace, a grandmother's scarf, or an old piece of jewelry. Something new signifies hope for the future and can be anything from a piece of clothing to a wedding band. Something borrowed is symbolic of future happiness and is often provided by a happily married friend of the bride. In ancient times, blue was the color of purity and often both the bride and the groom wore a band of blue cloth around the bottom of their wedding clothing. The knights of York gave us the Western European tradition of the groom wearing a single flower. It was customary for a knight to wear a flower or a colorful handkerchief belonging to their bride when they entered a tournament. The tradition later evolved to the groom wearing a flower from his bride's wedding bouquet.

The white wedding gown was not a symbol of purity, but rather a symbol of joy. What wedding today would be complete without a white wedding gown? Prior to the 16th century, however, this tradition was not common. Ann of Brittany popularized the white wedding dress in 1499.

During the Tudor period in England, it became customary for the wedding party to throw old shoes at the bride and groom's carriage. If the carriage was struck by a shoe, it was considered a symbol of good fortune to follow. From this old Western European wedding custom was born the tradition of strapping shoes to the back of the bride and groom's car.

What wedding tradition would be complete without the groom carrying his new bride over the threshold of their home? This Western European tradition began with two beliefs. The first one was that if the bride were to trip or stumble as she entered her new home, bad luck would plague the marriage. The second belief was that evil spirits inhabited the threshold of a new couple's home and that if the bride stepped on the threshold, the evil would enter through her feet and the marriage would be doomed.

The romantic answer, of course, was for the groom to carry his new bride across the threshold.

Western European wedding traditions have been passed down to us from many countries and cultures to blend into the romantic wedding traditions that we know and cherish today.

Chapter 5a

How Western European Tradition Affected African Christianity

*W*hen Christianity began in Africa, so many lifestyles and traditions were introduced into the African church by Europeans. And one of the traditions introduced to the African Church was the European wedding tradition, which has been explained in detail above.

Another was the dressing of the African-Christian, which was a cloth wrap around the body in a certain style called the African cultural attire with African sandals, became like that of the European who was wearing a shirt suit and tie. There was a general thought that the African-Christian dresses the European way since Christianity was Europeanized and not Africanized. Hence, one had to dress as such in order to qualify to be a Christian. This went to the extent that people were not recognized as Christians without European outfits, neither were people taken notice of when they wore African cultural attires to church.

I want to mention a true story of a situation related to how the European tradition of dressing affected African Christianity, although this story is not about marriage

directly. When my husband's uncle and godfather grad-
uated from Bible school to become a priest, he was supposed to give a final speech, so he decided to wear his
African *Kente* for his speech. The *Kente* is a very formal
African–Ghanaian outfit used for grand occasions. So yes,
he wore his *Kente* alright but unfortunately, he did not
receive a passing certificate. According to the regulations
of the Bible institute, he was not in formal attire—a suit
and tie. The bible school was run by European Christians
and although the institution was in Africa-Ghana, the
students were still required to wear European outfits as
a requirement for a passing certificate, among others. As
such he joined the Ghana army instead. He was Major
General and Chief of Defense Staff (CDS) during the time
of President Osagyefo Dr. Kwame Nkrumah, the first president of Ghana after independence.

Following on with the European traditions adapted
into the African traditions, the African Christian marriage
became a full observation of both the African traditional
marriage at home and a full white gown European wedding
style in Church, the only exclusion is the carrying of the
new bride across the threshold.

Since the end of the eighteenth century, some African
Pentecostal Christians enforced that born-again believers
had to have a European-style wedding that included a
white gown, veil, cake cutting, and more in the church. It
was also required that a reception take place before the
marriage was accepted by the church. The traditional
marriage had to be conducted in full detail as well before

the European-style wedding. The Pentecostal Christian marriage scenario has always undermined the traditional African marriage. And so up until now, what goes on with most African Pentecostal Christian marriages is that couples have two different types of marriage ceremonies which are the traditional African marriage and then the European-style marriage. In fact, the traditional marriage is less esteemed and not recognized as a marriage on its own unless a European-style wedding follows.

I cannot begin to state the detrimental effect this practice has had on marriages, and it is still practiced. About thirty-four years ago, I witnessed a church family meeting where there was confusion. A huge argument occurred between the reverend and leadership about a couple who had a traditional marriage but did not have enough money for a European-style wedding and reception. The couple lacked funds for a white gown and a cake, so they approached the reverend and expressed their situation. The reverend understood their financial situation and advised them to choose between the white gown and the cake, so the couple chose the cake. The reverend informed leadership and they would not bend their rules. If the couple could not afford both a white gown and a wedding cake, the marriage would not be recognized by church leadership. The reverend told leadership that he would bless the couple when they were ready, but leadership was in absolute disagreement. So the church family met to deliberate on church matters to help move the marriage forward. Some of the leadership decided to discuss the couple at the meeting and attack the reverend because they believed he was going to bless a couple who had not conformed to a marriage acceptable by the Pentecostal Church and, for that matter, unacceptable by God. You should have seen the ungodly and strange atmosphere that was formed in the church on that day.

During an African Pentecostal Church marriage, couples are told to stay away from each other after the traditional marriage has been performed. Sometimes, you are followed by a church steward to make sure you are staying away from each other.

Many couples are suspended, disciplined, and sometimes expelled from the church because they are seen together after their traditional African marriage and before their compulsory European-style wedding.

And if a woman becomes pregnant after her traditional marriage, but before her European-style wedding, shame and disgrace from the church alone is enough to destroy the couple's relationship and tear them apart. Most of the time, couples who are not strong enough to endure this attack give up their faith even.

A detailed study into this African Pentecostal Christian marriage scenario revealed certain factors that I believe led to this controversy.

The study showed these factors:

The mix-ups take place where the African Pentecostal Christians have placed the words *engagement*, *wedding*, and where *engagement ring* and *wedding ring* is used in the African-traditional marriage procedures.

The confusion starts with misuse of the word "engagement" in a traditional African marriage procedure. "Engagement" is used incorrectly in the third stage of the African traditional marriage process. The third stage of the African traditional marriage procedure is when the actual marriage takes place. But the African Pentecostal Christians call this stage engagement because at this stage the engagement ring is given to the bride instead of the wedding ring, even though the father of the bride pronounces his daughter as married to the groom. The wedding ring is given on the wedding day, which is the European-style wedding in the church building.

The word "engagement" has been used out of context for many years in the marriage procedures of the African Pentecostal Christians and this has caused and still causes troubles, debts, misunderstandings, divisions, confusions, and divorce.

In the European wedding tradition style, the engagement ring is used when the male promises to marry the female and so the engagement ring will seal the promise. At this point, there is no actual marriage.

In the African traditional marriage procedures, the *knocking of door* stage is the promising stage. So, if European wedding traditions are adapted, then the engagement ring must be used at the knocking of door stage.

The wedding ring must be used at the engagement stage of the traditional African marriage, which is equivalent to the wedding stage of the European wedding tradition where the bride is escorted down the aisle by her father and handed to the groom. This is when the wedding ring exchange takes place and the minister or bride's father pronounces the couple to be husband and wife.

I believe another mix up is the ceremony venue. The African Pentecostal Christian wants to believe that the marriage ceremony has to be in a church building or in a hall with church settings that include instruments in place, a choir, a pulpit, a minister, and a massive congregation. But the traditional African marriage is mostly performed in the family's home, hence, in the eye of the African Pentecostal that is not marriage.

One more mix-up is that it appears that the African Pentecostal Christian tends to believe that a couple must have both the African traditional and European-style marriages in order to show off the family's wealth. So, when it comes to the European-style wedding, a lot of money is spent to show that the couple is rich and also to prove that that is what they believe to be the marriage. In fact, this showing off of riches has led to weddings becoming more of a competition in the African Pentecostal Christian denominations. This has resulted in most couples financially stretching themselves more than they can afford.

In the Bible, the book of Hosea, fourth chapter and the sixth verse, God said His people are destroyed for lack of knowledge. He said because mankind has rejected knowledge, He God also will reject mankind from being His priest. Since we have forgotten the law of our God, He also will forget our children. The marriage looses value, respect, and is destroyed if the wedding becomes a competition because it creates all sorts of struggles right from the beginning of the marriage. The priests who knows that any one of these two marriage types—that is the African traditional and the European-style wedding—is good enough but encourages these two types of marriage ceremonies to be observed rather than supporting people to choose one type, has deviated from the genuine truth of God's Word.

I have officiated weddings and blessed couples who've only had £200 to spend, and I have also officiated weddings for couples who had more than £5000 to spend. I personally believe that the marriage itself is not about the financial, physical, or material things involved in a wedding ceremony, but is about the fulfillment of righteousness. What this means is that when people believe they must marry, (male and female, of course) they must be supported and guided in accordance with what God has instituted which makes marriage honorable, righteous, pure and beautiful. It is without pressure, and it is the physical symbol of how Christ Jesus is married to the church. Proverbs 18:22 (KJV) states, "Whoso findeth a wife findeth a good thing, and obtaineth favour of the Lord." For us pastors, bishops, and church leaders Proverbs 27:23 (KJV) states, "Be thou diligent to know the state of thy flocks and look well to thy herds."

Let us be careful therefore, to seek the wellbeing of the flock which the Lord has entrusted to us and be interested in their finding favor with the Lord rather than with us. For if in their sincere efforts to serve God righteously, the flock are victimized by wrongs, self-centered, and human rudiments of their leaders who they look up to, then the house of God has become a house of deception. Leaders, pastors, and bishops who know what is right but because they enjoy to see the flock lacking knowledge and succumbing to their manipulations and who are also using the church for their own personal gain, will not teach the flock the truth. For that matter, some flocks have become unknowingly bound mentally, psychologically, socially, and morally. No wonder the Bible says, in First Peter, chapter four, and the seventeenth verse that the time is come that judgement must begin at the house of God and if it begin at us, what shall the end be of them that obey not the gospel of God?

A while ago, I encountered a nice, African woman in my church. She approached me and said she wanted an appointment. Before then, whenever I saw the woman in church, I felt she was burdened with something and so I prayed for her.

The day came for our appointment, and she arrived at my office, sat down, and started crying. I asked if all her family members were okay. I asked her about work and her life in general. She answered all was well. So, I asked why she was crying. She said she wanted to confess her sins. I let her know we did not do that in our church. She said she knew that but still wanted me to hear her out. She said the reason why she came to church all by herself without her partner was because they were living in fornication and were not worthy to be in church. She tried to come, but her partner would not attend because he believed they were sinning.

I asked why her partner thought they were sinning. She said they were engaged and had completed all the necessary African traditional marriage procedures but they were not wedded in the church, so they were told by the pastor back home that they were living in sin and would face the wrath of God.

On that day, the Lord used me to educate and empower that beautiful woman who had been deceived and humiliated by the church. The chains of needless guilt, shame, and leader's philosophy was broken off her and she was liberated mentally, spiritually physically to enjoy her life, her marriage, and her husband.

The African Pentecostal Christian must establish that the *will* of God is bestowed on every marriage that is in accordance with the word of God. So whether the ceremony is at home or in a church building it makes no difference to the validity and the will of God concerning the marriage. Instead of questioning the physical elements of a wedding ceremony as to venues, buildings, ornaments, riches, and so on, church leaders should investigate:

- Have proper searches been made about each of couple regarding their background medically, socially?
- Is the marriage in accordance with divine principles, that is, is the marriage between male and female?

- Are the procedures biblical? That is have families been involved and is the bride's family satisfied with presentations from the groom family?
- Is the bride's father happy to give his daughter into marriage?
- Does the couple want to go a traditional marriage way or adopt a European-style marriage ceremony?
- Is the spirit of God leading the supporters to support the marriage to fulfill the will of God

If we can establish these facts, then the marriage is divine because marriage itself is an institution set up by God and, therefore, the only way marriage can succeed is to apply God's principle. Marriage is not about the outward displays of nice arrangements and crowd and pretty cars and so on that the church had made marriage to be in this present age. It is simply what God has said in His Word about marriage. Any other understanding besides what God's word says is a total deviation from the truth of God. The Bible says, in the book of Matthew, chapter eighteen, verse twenty that where two or three are gathered in His name, He is right there in their midst. And so Christians need to be bold and confident to walk in the will of God as He is with us always.

Pastors must support aspiring couples with prayer and sound biblical teachings. Couples need to know, beyond any reasonable doubt what a Godly marriage is.

I know of a couple who had resented the church because of how badly the church treated them when they were making marriage arrangements to the extent that they were pronounced sinful by the church. The couple were wise and knew exactly what to do, but the church had a problem with that. They knew the Pentecostals sometimes waste time and money, which created unnecessary tensions.

So the couple chose a traditional marriage, and that was it. After a while, God blessed them with a child. While they were overwhelmed with deep joy and gratitude to God, the church rose against them, saying the couple had not married at all and have committed sin by given birth. What? The reason was simple. The couple had a very decent African-traditional marriage in the bride's family home then her father declared them husband and wife and blessed them. However, since they did not follow this with a European-style ceremony in the church with white gown, veil, best man, bridesmaids, and so on, the Pentecostal church they attended refused to acknowledge their marriage. This is so sad.

Chapter 6

Temperaments and Personality Types

The spiritual personality and moral likeness of God in mankind have diverse manifestations in every individual by way of behavior, perceptions, aspirations, and thoughts. And these differences in mankind portrays all-wise and all-knowing beautiful abilities of God showing in all His creation. Imagine a world where everyone does things the same way? How boring would that be?

Temperament is the tendency to display certain special forms of behavior, which shapes us to become the person that we are, and so temperament can also be called Personality Type.

The theory of temperaments and personality types was first developed in the 460–377 B.C. by a Greek physician-philosopher. He identified four basic personalities: sanguine, melancholy, choleric, and phlegmatic.

In terms of understanding both you and the people around you, one of the most powerful tools at your disposal is understanding the underlying motivation behind each personality's behavior. Understanding your own motivations will help you to be more realistic in how you perceive life. In other words, if you understand your personality type, you will be more realistic when you think of life in view of, will life always be fun or perfect or under control or easy? Recognizing your personality type will enable you to adjust your expectations and keep your frustration level to a minimum.

Almost everyone you meet is motivated by a desire for life to be fun, perfect, under control, or easy. Once you understand a person's primary motivation, you can communicate with them on their terms, which will help them be more inclined to respond favorably to you.

A look at each personality type

- Sanguine: This type wants to have fun and be loved. When dealing with this type of person, ask yourself, "How can I make this more fun?"
- Melancholy: This type wants to bring perfection to an imperfect world, so ask yourself, "How can I do this in an orderly fashion?"
- Choleric: This type wants to control as much of his or her world as possible, so ask yourself, "How can I give this person a sense of ownership in this situation?"
- Phlegmatic: This type wants life to be easy and live in peace. To make the most of your relationship with this person, ask yourself, "How can I promote harmony in this situation?"

In marriage, both parties exhibit one or more of these personality types, but in order for temperaments to work best in building and beautifying the marriage one's personality type must be opposite the other's for a balanced, healthy, and peaceful relationship. This is because two kings cannot rule one empire.

So, while we are still naturally dominating and ruling, we need to allow the Holy Spirit to enable us to control our temperaments so they complement each other. By so doing, who we truly are will become a blessing to each other because we become authentic in all our ways, no hidden agendas, no bondage, only liberation. We become just as the Bible says in the book of Philippians, chapter four and verse thirteen, that we can do all things through Christ Jesus who strengthens us.

There are certain scenarios, however, where a person may exhibit contrasting personalities. A person's character may not be what they truly are. They act differently to who they really are. This may happen if a child experienced overpowering parents who forced the child to become something they were not. Or, perhaps, certain occurrences took place along the way that changed them and remolded them into someone different.

Perhaps birth order plays a major role in a person exhibiting a contrasting personality. For example: the first-born child had a sanguine personality but the parents worked day and night to make the child a melancholy, so the child ended up demonstrating many melancholy traits. Or the last born child is a choleric but parents wanted a phlegmatic personality child and so they trained the child to exhibit phlegmatic traits. Furthermore, a person may imitate a mentor of a trainer or someone else who they admire and may end up just like the one they imitate rather than being who they really are.

The key to your self-understanding and freedom that will make you begin to excel as the real you is to get back in touch with who you were as a child. Look at who you are when you are at your absolute best and identify what you do. That is the ultimate you and the personality you exhibit.

What if a person is a little bit of each personality type? Well, that could mean:

+ You are spiritually mature and well-balanced in all areas of life. You know how to kick back and have a great time, but you also know when to take life seriously. You know when it is appropriate to take charge of the situation, but you are not a king in diplomacy. If you have walked in a close relationship with God for many years, you have become a reflection of Him. Just as the Bible says in the book of Ephesians, chapter five, verses one and two that we should imitate God, therefore, in everything we do, because we are His dear children. And that we should live lives filled with love, following the example of Christ. He loved us and offered himself as a sacrifice for us, a pleasing aroma to God.

+ You have the ability to exercise self-control and are able to demonstrate different types of personality when faced with different situations.
+ You might have multiple personality disorder. This is a type of disease or demon-possession situation that might need medical or spiritual attention.

Chapter 7

Excellence of Love

There are different forms and styles of love. To describe these styles, the Ancient Greeks created four terms: *agape, philia, storge, and eros.*

Agape

Agape is an unconditional love that sees beyond the outer surface and accepts the recipient for who they are, regardless of their flaws, shortcomings, or faults. It is the type of love that everyone must strive to have for everyone. Even if you do not like someone, you decide to love them. This kind of love is about sacrifice, as well as giving and expecting nothing in return. The translation of the word *agape* is love in the verb form meaning, *love* is a doing word. It is the love demonstrated by one's behavior toward another person. It is a committed and chosen love. This is the love that Jesus demonstrated to us.

Phileo

Phileo love refers to an affectionate, warm, and tender platonic love. It makes you desire friendship with someone. It is the kind of love which livens up the agape love. Although you may have an agape love for your enemies, you may not have a phileo love for the same people. The translation of the word phileo is love in the noun-form. It is how you feel about someone. It is a committed and chosen love.

Storge

Storge is a family and friendship type of love. It is the love that parents naturally feel for their children, the love family members have for each other, or the love friends have for each other. In some cases, this friendship love may turn into a romantic relationship, and the couple in such a relationship becomes best friends. Storge love is unconditional, accepts flaws or faults, and ultimately drives you to forgive. It is committed, sacrificial, and makes you feel secure, comfortable, and safe.

Eros

Eros is a passionate and intense love that arouses romantic feelings. It is the kind that often triggers *high feelings* in a new relationship and makes you say, "I love you." It is an emotional and sexual love. Although this romantic love is important in the beginning of a new relationship, it may not last unless it is directed more towards the other person because it focuses more on self. If the person in love does not feel good about their relationship anymore, they will stop loving their partner.

This list offers you a general understanding and description of the four types of love that promote a good, healthy, and progressive relationship. In any relationship, you should have all four loves working together. But in some cases, a relationship may be long-lasting if partners share the same style of love.

God demonstrated unconditional agape love, as an example for mankind to follow, as in the book of Ephesians mentioned above. Again, God so loved the world that He gave His only begotten Son, that whoever believes in Him shall not perish, but have eternal life. For God did not send the Son into the world to judge the world, but that the world might be saved through Him. And by this love, He commissions mankind to love one another and to continue in His love. God's commandment about love is that we love one another, just as He has loved us. Greater love has no one than this, that one lay down his life for his friends. He said we are His friends if we do what He commands us. Bible reference John 15:12–14 (KJV).

God commended his love toward us, in that, while we were yet sinners, Christ died for us. Bible reference Romans 5:8 (KJV).

Apostle Paul continued to talk about agape love saying if you speak with the tongues of men and of angels, but do not have love, you have become a noisy gong or a clanging cymbal. If you have the gift of prophecy and know all mysteries and all knowledge; and if you have all faith, so as to remove mountains, but do not have love, you are nothing. And if you give all your possessions to feed the poor, and surrender your body to be burned, but do not have love, it profits nothing.

Love is patient, love is kind and is not jealous; love does not brag and is not arrogant, does not act unbecomingly; it does not seek its own, is not provoked, does not take into account a wrong suffered, does not rejoice in unrighteousness, but rejoices with the truth; bears all things, believes all things, hopes all things, endures all things. Love never fails.

If there are gifts of prophecy, they will be done away; if there are tongues, they will cease; if there is knowledge, it will be done away but love remains forever. I Corinthians 13(KJV).

Unconditional love is the foundation and the platform on which God established this divine institution of marriage. The functionality, success, and beauty of marriage lie in the measure of love within it. Love will allow people to accept each other just as they are. Love will establish true communication. Love will build trust. Love will remove all cultural and traditional barriers. Love will endure. Love will forgive. Love will persevere. Love will not let go. Love will have compassion. Love is merciful. Love is righteous. Love is more important than money. Love cares. Love gives. Love builds up. Love will not destroy. Love creates. Love makes the impossible possible. Love is union. Love is one accord.

The Tower of Babel was becoming successful because God said the people were with one accord, so anything was possible to them. In the beginning of age, according to the book of Genesis, chapter eleven, verses one to six, the whole earth used the same language and the same words. It came about as the people of Babel journeyed eastward, they found a plain in the land of Shinar and settled there.

They said to one another, "Come, let us make bricks and burn them thoroughly." And they used brick for stone, and they used tar for mortar. They said, "Come, let us build for ourselves a city, and a tower whose top will reach into heaven, and let us make for ourselves a name, otherwise we will be scattered abroad over the face of the whole earth." The Lord came down to see the city and the tower which the sons of men had built. The Lord said, "Behold, they are one people, and they all have the same language. And this is what they began to do, and now nothing which they purpose to do will be impossible for them."

There is no limitation to love, there is an achievement with love and God expects us to love one another. Therefore endeavor to love one another in marriage: for love is of God and everyone that loves is born of God and knows God. Where there is no love in the marriage, it means that God's love does not exist in the union. But God manifested His love toward us because He sent his only begotten Son into the world, that we might live through Him. So herein is love, not that we loved God, but that He loved us, and sent His Son to be the propitiation for our sins. If God so loved us, we ought also to love one another. No man has seen

God at any time but if we love one another, God dwells in us and his love is perfected in us.

Further scriptures that describe the love that God wants couples to share in marriage are:

Ephesians 4:2–3 (KJV) states, "With all lowliness and meekness, with longsuffering, forbearing one another in love; Endeavoring to keep the unity of the Spirit in the bond of peace."

Colossians 3:14 (KJV) states, "And above all these things put on charity, which is the bond of perfectness."

Romans 13:8 (KJV) states, "Owe no man anything, but to love one another: for he that loveth another hath fulfilled the law."

Chapter 8

Disputes, Misunderstandings, and Resolutions in Marriage

My study on the subject of marriage has taught me that, most often, couples notice different things about each other immediately after they get married. These new discoveries may pose serious problems for the marriage. Sometimes, these things do not surface due to lack of counseling or medical examinations, or simply not deeply enquiring into family backgrounds before the marriage.

Some people realize after they get married, their partner has dyslexia, is schizophrenic, or has a terminal illness. They may even realize their partner has other financial obligations that can put a strain on the marriage.

These are not grounds for divorce, but if they are not handled or dealt with, they can lead to unhealthy, unhappy marriages full of resentment, anger, and confusion, and then divorce. When such perplexities happen, partners tend to conclude that things cannot be fixed, and they would be better off going opposite directions due to their inability to deal with the situation. But when we refer to Jesus's words in the Bible, specifically, the book of Matthew 19:26 (KJV), when His disciples were wondering who could be saved. He said unto them, "With men this is impossible; but with God all things are possible." So if the situation is handled by turning it over to Jesus, then there is no such thing as, it cannot be fixed, it is out of control, it is too late, or we have come to our wit's end and there is nothing we can do. The Lord is expecting us to bring all our burdens to Him and then have faith and trust Him to help us resolve them rather than making conclusions and running away from our burdens.

So yes, shocking discoveries after marriage can occur, but we must look at them all through God's perspective. The only way that mankind will have long and satisfying life is to never forget the ordinances and precepts of God and so when it comes to marriage, it is important that couples keep marriage ordinances set up by God who instituted marriage. And if we let the marriage be shaped by integrity and truth of the word of God, we will find favor and understanding with God and with each other. Then we will have a full, rewarding marriage life

- Let us say you found out that your partner had trouble with reading despite normal intelligence, and you did not notice this. Neither were you told before the marriage. Dyslexia is a common learning difficulty that can cause problems with reading, writing, and spelling. Unlike a learning disability, intelligence is not affected. The partner with dyslexia should not feel ashamed of this but humbly apologize and admit that there is an issue and then be willing to ask for support. It is there and then the process to resolve the problem can begin, with both partners working together to look for support such as information on dyslexia and consulting the rights places and people for help.

+ If you discover your partner is schizophrenic or has any form of illness, encourage your partner to seek proper treatment and then, take things one step at a time.

+ If you find out your partner is in debt or has financial obligations outside your relationship, try working together to create a plan to be debt free. If it works, great! Otherwise, seek counseling and advice from specialists and work with them to help you come out of debt or help you fulfill those financial obligations which cast negative effects on a marriage.

These suggestions apply to any problems that arise after the wedding and during the marriage. When frustration begins to set in, call on God from whom our help will come. He is the one who made heaven and earth. He will not suffer your foot to be moved and He will not slumber at all. Let the Lord be your keeper and your shade upon your right hand and no harm can ever befall you. Even the moon cannot smite you by day or by night. The Lord shall preserve you from all evil: He shall preserve your soul. The Lord shall preserve your going out and your coming in all the days of your life and through your marriage and it shall be well. Absolutely nothing can be against you.

You can also seek godly counsel from your bishop, pastor, or good friends.

Having said all that, I believe the best and proper scenario, though is that couples will be sincere and open up with each other before they get married and talk through any major issues they know of. Do blood tests and medical examinations, make necessary enquiries about each other's families and where they come from. See if there is any detrimental information that you cannot handle. And then let these factors form a good part of your decision making into the union with each other. That way, you are not bound to take on any responsibility that might tamper with your joy and liberty.

If you still choose to enter into matrimony, then of course, you are both ready for whatever situations you may face. Some of the information you find may even be resolvable before the marriage, which will also bring ease of mind to go into the marriage.

I remember I counseled a couple before their marriage, and I asked them to do a blood test—this is just part of my usual counseling procedures. They found that the lady had cervical cancer and at an early stage. She started to treat this and with much prayers as well, she was healed completely. In their ten years of marriage, now they have four children. Hallelujah and amen! The Bible says that he who finds a wife finds a good thing and obtains favor of the Lord. And so when God blesses a man with wisdom and direction to find a wife, it is both partner's responsibility to make sure who they found is of good physical and spiritual health so the finding of each other opens doors to God's favor into the union.

Now, let us talk about a scenario involving mistakes. When two different people, with individual differences, come together, there will be times the couple will not see eye to eye on issues. This is expected. Our Sovereign Lord even calls us to come and reason together with Him in times that we misunderstand Him and in times that our sins are as scarlet and red as crimson. He said when we reason with Him, He will cleanse us to become as white as snow and wool. If God calls His people to come and reason with Him, then couples can also reason with each other in times when there are misunderstandings. This is when strong and effective communication must come in. It is key to building habits of trust and faithfulness with each other and thereby, know each other better. So do not keep quiet about issues and think they will go away. Talk about everything and anything: how you feel, your plans, who you talk to often, what happens at work, your interests, hobbies, fears, weaknesses, likes, and dislikes, strengths, everything. Be incredibly open and plain with each other, yet remain respectful. When the Bible says the two become one, it means you are taking good care of each other to take good care of yourself as you mold the other to become just like you.

When you experience disputes and misunderstandings, seek God first and try to amicably resolve things. Our Lord

God calls us to come to Him with all our burdens and troubles that are weighing us down and He will give us rest. And so it does not matter what the confusion, frustration, or misunderstanding is, there is always a way out. So I encourage couples, by the name of our Lord Jesus Christ, that they will agree, and that there be no division among them but that they should be perfectly joined together in the same mind and in the same judgment. Indeed, our Lord Jesus is able to help us through our burdens. He will grant grace, wisdom, and favor to those who seek Him and enable them to live humbly with each other and work to resolve whatever brings the confusion and misunderstandings. And the Lord God will bless you, and keep you, make his face shine upon you and be gracious unto you. The Lord will lift His countenance upon you and give you peace to live a victorious and successful married life. There is absolutely nothing He cannot do.

The Bible tells that the grace of the Lord Jesus Christ and the love of God and the communion of the Holy Ghost will be with us always. So as the couple seeks God in times of misunderstandings, God will be gracious to them and enable the Holy Spirit to help them through the situation. The Holy Spirit may also direct the couple to invite a third party into the situation, someone to mediate for them so they can express their views to each other peacefully. So a counselor or a trusted friend or the pastor or bishop may come in to support them with godly counsel and biblical support to help their union to refresh and get stronger rather than tearing apart.

A biblical reference is Matthew 18:15–16 (KJV), "Moreover if thy brother shall trespass against thee, go and tell him his fault between thee and him alone. If he shall hear thee, thou hast gained thy brother. But if he will not hear thee, then take with thee one or two more, that in the mouth of two or three witnesses every word may be established."

Chapter 9

The Grounds for Divorce and Remarriage

$\mathcal{M}$arriage is divinely designed by God as a physical symbol of the spiritual marriage of Christ Jesus and the Church. Revelations 19:7–8 (NASB) states, "Let us rejoice and be glad and give the glory to Him, for the marriage of the Lamb has come and His bride has made herself ready. It was given to her to clothe herself in fine linen, bright and clean; for the fine linen is the righteous acts of the saints." Just as Christ, the groom, is the head of the Church which is the bride, so is the husband the head of his wife.

Our Lord and Saviour Jesus Christ encourages wives to be subject to their own husbands, as to the Lord. For the husband is the head of the wife, as Christ also is the head of the church, He Himself being the Saviour of the church. But as the church is subject to Christ, so also the wives ought to be subject to their husbands in everything. Husbands must love their wives, just as Christ also loved the church and gave Himself up for her. This is so He might sanctify her, having cleansed her by the washing of water with the word, that He might present to Himself the church in all her glory, having no spot or wrinkle or any such thing; but that she would be holy and blameless.

So husbands ought also to love their own wives as their own bodies. He who loves his own wife loves himself; for no one ever hated his own flesh, but nourishes and cherishes it, just as Christ also does the church, because we are members of Christ's body.

Isaiah 54:5 (KJV) states, "For thy Maker is thine husband; the Lord of hosts is his name; and thy Redeemer the Holy One of Israel; The God of the whole earth shall he be called."

This Divine Institution is a Great Mystery

You see if the church divorced Christ, the whole order and plan of God's divine institution, which is the church as the bride and Christ as the bridegroom demonstrated in humanity through the marriage institution between a husband and wife, is nullified. Therefore, the blessings that come with the marriage institution is removed, and a vacuum is created, which allows everything opposite blessings to occupy this vacuum, causing a detrimental effect. If there is divorce between a man and wife, the consequences of the divorce extends beyond the couple. It becomes a situation of a generational negative (anti-Christ) cycle effect that extends through families besides the pain, bitterness, resentment and so on that accompanies the divorce. It devastates, tears apart and breaks children and if people don't seek the grace of God for divine intervention through intensive prayers to break this negative generational cycle the divorce brings, it creates a pattern that repeats itself over and over.

God hates divorce. Malachi 2:14–16 (NASB) states, "Yet you say, 'For what reason?' Because the Lord has been a witness between you and the wife of your youth, against whom you have dealt treacherously, though she is your companion and your wife by covenant. But no one has done so who has a remnant of the Spirit. And what did that one do while he was seeking a godly offspring? 'Take heed then to your spirit and let no one deal treacherously against the wife of your youth. For I hate divorce,' says the Lord, the God of Israel, 'and him who covers his garment with wrong,' says the Lord of hosts. 'So take heed to your spirit that you do not deal treacherously.'"

The Bible further records in Matthew chapter nineteen that Jesus departed from Galilee and came into the region of Judea beyond the Jordan and large crowds followed Him, and He healed them there. But some Pharisees came to Jesus, testing Him and asking, "Is it lawful for a man to divorce his wife for any reason at all?" And Jesus answered and said, "Have you not read that He who created them from the beginning made them male and female and said, for this reason a man shall leave his father and mother and be joined to his wife and the two shall become one flesh? So they are no longer two, but one flesh. What therefore God has joined together, let no man separate." The Pharisees asked Jesus, "Why then did Moses command to give her a certificate of divorce and send her away?" Jesus said to them, "Because of your hardness of heart, Moses permitted you to divorce your wives, but from the beginning it has not been this way." And Jesus continued to say to them whoever divorces his wife, except for immorality, and marries another woman has committed adultery.

Divorce, on many grounds, has existed since the time of Moses. People in the Old Testament days forced Moses to permit them to divorce by issuing a certificate of divorce, and so, putting on weight was a good enough grounds for divorce as it was committing adultery.

And in these modern times, the norm is irreconcilable differences, as soon as a couple feels they do not agree with each other on most things or they are not coming to an amicable place with important matters, it is good enough grounds for divorce. I mean, divorce has become that easy and simple. Therefore, it is important I iterate the precautions of divorce. Jesus said, plainly, that whoever divorces his wife and marries another woman commits adultery against her, and if she divorces her husband and marries another man, she is committing adultery. Everyone who divorces his wife and marries another commits adultery, and he who marries one who is divorced from a husband commits adultery.

Since time began, there has been only one grounds for divorce, and that is adultery. But even adultery is forgivable by Jesus. The story is told in the Bible. In the book of John, chapter eight, and the first eleven verses, it tells of how early one morning Jesus came again into the temple to teach. And the scribes and Pharisees brought unto him a woman taken in adultery. When they had set her in the midst of the temple, they said to Jesus, "Master, this woman was taken in adultery, in the very act. Now, in the law Moses commanded us, that such should be stoned: but what do you say?" They said this because they were looking for something to accuse him of. But Jesus stooped down, and with his finger wrote on the ground, as though he did not hear them.

So when they continued asking him, he lifted up himself, and said unto them, "He that is without sin among you, let him first cast a stone at her." And again he stooped down, and wrote on the ground. And they which heard it, being convicted by their own conscience, went out one by one, beginning at the eldest, even unto the last: and Jesus was left alone, and the woman standing in the midst. When Jesus had lifted himself, and saw none but the woman, He said unto her, "Woman, where are those who accuse you? Has no man condemned you?"

She said, "No man, Lord." And Jesus said unto her, "Neither do I condemn you. Go, and sin no more." This Jesus demonstrated to teach mankind that even adultery can be forgiven and anything else can be forgiven by couples themselves and so we have the choice.

Divorce can still be avoided if we choose to work at life's demands from our Maker's point of view and be kind one to another, tenderhearted, forgiving one another, even as God for Christ's sake hath forgiven us. Likewise, husbands must dwell with their wives according to knowledge, honoring them, and regarding them as being heirs together of the grace of life, so that husbands' prayers will not be hindered. For if we forgive men their trespasses, our heavenly Father will also forgive us, but if we do not forgive men their trespasses, neither will our Father forgive us our trespasses.

Furthermore, we must forbear one another and forgive one another if anyone has a quarrel against any, even as Jesus Christ forgave us, so also we must do. And above all these things, we must put on charity, which is the bond of perfectness. So with all lowliness and meekness, with long-suffering, forbearing one another in love, we must endeavor to keep the spirit of unity in the bond of peace, trusting in the Lord with all our heart and not leaning on our own understanding but acknowledging our Lord God in all our ways, so He will make our paths straight removing every and any struggles from our way. And above all things, having fervent love among ourselves for love shall cover the multitude of sins.

See how beautifully King Solomon puts it in the book of Song of Solomon 8:6-7? I quote from the Kings James version, "Set me as a seal upon thine heart, as a seal upon thine arm: for love is strong as death; jealousy is cruel as the grave: the coals thereof are coals of fire, which hath a most vehement flame. Many waters cannot quench love, neither can the floods drown it: if a man would give all the substance of his house for love, it would utterly be contemned."

This king knew that where there is love, there is peace, strength; there is togetherness, there is power and so it is worthwhile to give all the substance of one's house for love. A person standing alone can be attacked and defeated, but two can stand back-to-back and conquer. Three are even better, for a triple-braided cord is not easily broken. Love is fortified strength.

There are two ways of looking at the demands of our lives. We can see the demands as problems or as challenges we can overcome. Part of maturing is recognizing that challenges will contain problems. The man or woman who becomes truly fruitful and prosperous learns, with God's help, what to do about problems.

Jesus sees our present troubles as small and something that does not last awfully long, yet they produce for us a glory that vastly outweighs problems and will last forever. So we must not look at the troubles, rather, we fix our gaze on Jesus, who knows the end from the beginning to help us go through our present problems. That way we overcome and benefit from the outcome of what we go through. For the things we see now will soon be gone, but the things we cannot see will last forever.

We should note that as long as we are two unique people with individual differences and opinions in the marriage, we may not always see things the same, therefore problems are inevitable. However, problems are hurdles to be overcome and not to be looked at as some unsolvable situations and as such must be overwhelmed by. Hence, if we stop magnifying our problems in our marriages and start magnifying the marriage in accordance with God's perspective as a place of endless learning where two completely different personalities are together to reflect the mystery in God's institution, the marriage life will be very enjoyable. There will be meaning to the marriage life, good health, longevity, and prosperousness for both the couple and for the family unit, which will extend to generations to come because Jesus will be the center of it all.

Some also believe that separation is an option when the marriage is not working. As a matter of fact, I have heard some pastors and bishops talk about separation and referring to a scripture which Apostle Paul mentioned in 1 Corinthians 7:2-5. I quote from the New Living Translation.

> But because there is so much sexual immorality, each man should have his own wife, and each woman should have her own husband. The husband should fulfill his wife's sexual needs, and the wife should fulfill her husband's needs. The wife gives authority over her body to her husband, and the husband gives authority over his body to his wife. Do not deprive each other of sexual relations unless you both agree to refrain from sexual intimacy for a limited time so you can give yourselves more completely to prayer. Afterward, you should come together again so that Satan will not be able to tempt you because of your lack of self-control.

This separation Paul talks about is not for when there are disagreements. Instead, he refers to a time that both couples will agree to set aside to pray fast and seek the face of God fervently for just a short time. This time of separation in prayer should not be so long to give Satan a chance to sneak into the marriage. However, most people of God talk about separation as if it is biblical and all right. But, they have twisted the interpretation of this scripture and dwell on it to separate from their spouse and marital homes for years, and they believe it is okay. Apostle Paul went on to say in further verses of the same chapter above that, "But for those who are married, I have a command that comes not from me, but from the Lord. A wife must not leave her husband. But if she does leave him, let her remain single or else be reconciled to him. And the husband must not leave his wife."

Grounds for Remarriage

According to the Bible, a widow should remarry. This is according to Timothy 5:14 (NASB), which says, "Therefore, I want younger widows to get married, bear children, keep house, and give the enemy no occasion for reproach." A widow can be either the male or the female whose better half has passed on, and the Bible is saying in order not to be consumed in lust and in yielding to temptation of fornication or in any way for the devil to criticize you, it is good that you remarry.

The Victim in the Divorce

The Apostle Paul gave these instructions about the victim in the divorce to the church of Christ in the same scripture as quoted earlier from Corinthians. Here, I quote from verses 12-17.

> Now, I will speak to the rest of you, though I do not have a direct command from the Lord. If a fellow believer has a wife who is not a believer and she is willing to continue living with him, he must not leave her. And if a believing woman has a husband who is not a believer and he is willing to continue living with her, she must not leave him. For the believing wife brings holiness to her marriage, and the believing husband brings holiness to his marriage. Otherwise, your children would not be holy, but now they are holy. But if the husband or wife who is not a believer insists on leaving, let them go. In such cases the believing husband or wife is no longer bound to the other, for God has called you to live in peace. Don't you wives realize that your husbands might be saved because of you? And don't you husbands realize that your wives might be saved because of you? Each of you should continue to live in whatever situation the Lord has placed you

and remain as you were when God first called you. This is my rule for all the churches.

In summary, Apostle Paul says the young widows can remarry and a believer who has been divorced by their non-believing spouse can also remarry. But if the non-believing spouse is willing to keep the believing partner then let the believing partner stay on in the marriage for the believing partner brings holiness into the marriage, and perhaps the non-believing partner might come to repentance and also believe. He goes on to advise that, if possible, let the marriage continue to remain as it was when one of the spouses became a believer.

Chapter 10

An Abusive Marriage

*B*ehavior can develop as a result of how a person was raised. Someone who becomes an abuser as an adult might have been abused at an early age or exposed to abuse. These children may start out as bullies in childhood then become dominating and controlling as adults. To them, a normal life might be controlling people against their will, bossing them around, and acting physically or verbally abusive to another.

The scenario of the abused may be same or similar. They may have picked up the attitude of accepting abuse from childhood, due to their perhaps seeing a parent or a family member or someone who influenced them. While growing up, they accept all the abuse as normal. They feel they are not loved unless they are abused, mistreated, and cursed at. They think they must accept abuse as part of life, so they settle for it and not be prepared to change their conditions.

In my personal observation through abusive marriages/ cases I have been part of, I find most abused people will never take a step to get help. This is because they are afraid, have become timid, and have settled for less. And unless someone intervenes and speaks to them to know that that kind of state they are in is abnormal, and by the grace of God the Lord opens their eyes to comprehend, they never try to find help. Otherwise, why would an abused person run back to their abuser and tell them how another person suggested they seek help? This happened in one case that I worked on. About sixty percent of murder cases in the U.K. are due to abuse. [1]Statistics on domestic abuse: Will affect 1 in 4 women and 1 in 6 men in their lifetime; Leads to, on average, two women being murdered each week and 30 men per year; Accounts for 16% of all violent crime (Source: Crime in England and Wales 04/05 report), however it is still the violent crime least likely to be reported to the police."

This is not the kind of life God has designed for mankind and for marriage at all. For God has set up good, blessed and pleasant plans for mankind right from the beginning of age, plans for welfare and not for calamity to give us a future and a hope.

No one should settle for abuse, for God has not given us a spirit of timidity, but of power and love and discipline. By His divine power, God has given us everything we need in order to live a decent and godly life. We receive all of this by coming to know Him, the one who calls us to himself by means of His marvelous glory and excellence. And because of His glory and excellence, He has given us great and precious promises. These are the promises that enable us to share his divine nature and escape the world's corruption caused by human desires. Spirit of timidity is a spirit that enables you to lack conviction, boldness, or courage. It makes you overly cautious or fearful, easily frightened, and/ or shy. Above all, the spirit of timidity damages one's emotions and lowers one's self esteem. If an abuser can get you to this place of damaged emotions and low self-esteem, then they have succeeded in their endeavor to destroy you. But this is not what God wants for anyone. And God has a way out of this.

God has given us power. The word power came out of the Greek word *dunamis*, which refers to strength or ability or moral power and excellence of soul. Most importantly, *dunamis* can refer to inherent power, power residing in a thing by virtue of its nature or power which a person or thing exerts and put forth.

We do not live a Christian life because of our own power. It is God's ability that makes us able to accomplish anything of virtue, for apart from Him, we can do nothing. He is the vine we are the branches. God's strength makes us overcomers. So, by virtue of the nature of God in man, we have the power of God in us.

God has given us love. He demonstrated His own love toward us when He gave Jesus to die on the cross. For God so loved the world, that He gave His only begotten Son, that whoever believes in Him shall not perish, but have eternal life. For Greater love has no one than this, that one lay down his life for his friends who have allowed Him to come into their lives to be their Lord and Savior. In the same way, if we have love, we will give our best gift to our lover as God has given His best gift to us. Furthermore, the Bible commands Christians to pursue righteousness, godliness, faith, love, steadfastness, and gentleness. Therefore husbands, live with your wives in an understanding way, showing honor and love to the woman since they are heirs with you of the grace of life, so that your prayers may not be hindered.

Therefore, all forms of physical, emotional, verbal, and sexual abuse are forbidden.

God gave us a spirit of discipline and a sound mind. Discipline is an art that requires knowledge, skill, sensitivity, and self-confidence. Like any art form, discipline is acquired through training and experience. It becomes easier with practice. Knowledge empowers a person to have common sense. Common sense will not support you when participating in the abuse of others or being abused. The application of empowered knowledge brings wisdom and wisdom brings sound mind. This will all make and achieve for you divine greatness in God.

Therefore, no one must allow themselves to be abused or become an instrument to abuse others. We have all been created in the image and likeness of God, according to Genesis 1:26 (NASB), which states, "Then God said, 'Let Us make man in Our image, according to Our likeness.'" So we have in us the ability to do good and show love toward one another and be disciplined in our conduct as people who are the moral likeness and spiritual personality of the most high God.

Know that we are fearfully and wonderfully made, according to Psalm 139:14 (NASB), which says, "I will give thanks to You, for I am fearfully and wonderfully made; Wonderful are Your works, And my soul knows it very well." Therefore, we do not need anyone's approval before we know we are precious in God's eyes. Many times, the abused starts down the path of abuse by always waiting on people's opinion on them or what they do, waiting to be praised and to be told they look good or beautiful or handsome. Otherwise, they are easily discouraged and cannot function and then they begin to live unconsciously of themselves such that they are ineffective without someone's (the abuser's) opinion. So the abuser sees an opportunity and sneak in, then escalate to the next step where the abuse is told what to wear, how to dress, oh you are too fat so cut your food portions, oh I like you to do things a certain way, and the list goes on nonstop. And before they realize the abuser has dominated them fully and then that useless lifestyle of an abusive relationship carries on.

If you are in an abusive relationship, please leave this relationship. Run from it. If you are engaged, break the engagement. Do not deceive yourself thinking that the abuser loves you and that he/she will change.

And If you are married and have been abused, please seek help immediately. Talk to a counselor or someone for support. Do not settle for a lie; abuse does not equal love. Abuse will only destroy you. Anything that comes to steal and kill and destroy is described in the Bible as a thief. And so do not be moved by where abuse is coming from, either from the bishop or the prince or the pauper—enough is enough. Jesus came that we would have life in its abundance and so whatever does not add progress and advancement and abundance to your life must not be accepted at all.

Sometimes even friends, coworkers, or neighbors can become abusive. It is especially important that you shun them and pray for them from a distance. Furthermore, to the person who has been abused, please know that the abuser is not the ultimate figure of power and authority in your life. God is the ultimate figure of power and authority in your life and it is not His will for you to be compelled against your will and so do not accept abuse at all.

Chapter 11

Childbearing and Adoption

*O*n the fifth day of creation, God commanded the water be filled with many kinds of living beings and for the air to be filled with birds. God created the great sea monsters, all kinds of creatures that live in the water, and all kinds of birds. He blessed them all and told the creatures that live in the water to reproduce and to fill the sea, and he told the birds to increase in number.

Then God commanded the earth to produce all kinds of animal life: domestic and wild, large, and small. And it was done. And He was pleased with what he saw. Afterward, God said to the Son and the Holy Spirit that they should make human beings who will have their moral personality and spiritual likeness and who will have power over the fish, the birds, and all animals, domestic and wild, large and small.

So God created human beings, making them to be like himself. He created them male and female, blessed them, and said to them, *Have many children, so that your descendants will live all over the earth and bring it under their control.*

God blessed men and women. He empowered them to be fruitful and multiply. And so it is only natural for a man and woman in marriage to bear children.

Sometimes though, due to a medical condition or other circumstances, they may not be able to have children of their own. So, they adopt children and love and raise them as their own. This is a perfectly normal, healthy, prosperous, and sensible decision. Furthermore, it is also okay for a single person to adopt, love, and care for a child. When you look at adoption from a divine perspective, we see how God sent Jesus to come and die for us due to His love for mankind, not willing that anyone should perish but that all men should come to repentance. Therefore He adopted into sonship those of us who were gentiles and believed, spiritually grafting us into His vineyard, and made us heirs of the Father even joint-heirs with the Son. And so physical adoption of a child continues to demonstrate and extend God's love.

Chapter 12

Same-Sex Couples and Adoption

When it comes to same-sex couples or partners adopting children, my opinion is to bring the scenario into alignment with the Word of God so we can see what the divine principle is surrounding adoption. In previous chapters, I have explained in detail how God does not favor same-sex unions because of how He made mankind from the beginning, male and female and commissioned them to join in matrimony and then be fruitful and multiply. Adoption can take place when, due to certain circumstances, a couple is unable to have children.

It could also be that a couple can physically have children but would still adopt more. Or a single person who loves children could also adopt. Siblings within one family sometimes adopts each other's children when there is death and so on. This is all good because the adoption of children is not limited to only when a couple cannot bear children of their own.

However, for a couple to adopt children, it will be more blessing for the simple divine principle as stated in the bible book of Genesis chapter two be considered. So adopting

THE *Marriage* INSTITUTION

couple in a heterosexual relationship is a good scenario of what God instituted to be a healthy and proper environment for a child to grow, hence, the adopted child. If a single male or female is adopting, he or she must simply be the beautiful original authentic creation of God, if male, naturally exhibiting masculine gender qualities and if female, exhibiting natural feminine gender qualities as made by God. You see, God has a perfect plan for humanity all through generations. That is why He placed His morale likeness and spiritual personality in man, in order that mankind will have qualities and abilities. Some will appear just in males and some just in females. What I mean to say is that God has given certain qualities that only males can exhibit and certain qualities for only females to exhibit and this supports, builds, and empowers society.

With an adoption, these qualities are necessary for a child to grow, develop, and be equipped to be part of society, naturally. Any exposure to the child contrary to God's wonderous creation of male and female and how we function uniquely and naturally will hinder the child from knowing and recognizing and acknowledging and understanding the beautiful purpose and plan of God's creation. God commissions parents to train up a child the way they should go, teaching them to seek God's wisdom and God's will for their abilities and talents, so that even when they are grown, they will not depart from God's wisdom.

So you see, when we look at the divine perspective of a same-sex couple adopting children, it is obvious that, while same-sex parents have the same natural functions and abilities, the child will be seriously lacking. The child will be denied divinely-arranged functions and abilities necessary in the home for their development—naturally, spiritually, physically, and progressively.

I believe the origination of all the confusion in the world today regarding marriage, adoption, and lifestyles are rooted from what the Bible describes as the battle of the anti-Christ. You see, in ancient times, things like homosexuality, same-sex couples, same-sex adoptions and many other situations as explained in detail in previous chapters, were hidden and not spoken of openly at all. It was because they were termed as *abominable iniquity* eschewed by God and were subject to immediate death when brought to light.

As the world population expanded and civilization and modernization advanced the anti-Christ, who is Satan, also intensified his strategies of deception. And so, just like in the Garden of Eden, where Satan first succeeded in deceiving Eve to eat of the fruit of the tree of knowledge of good and evil, while God told Adam and Eve not to eat of it, in the same way he began to fight against God by deceiving humanity to bring out and accept some things that were eschewed by God, in his attempt to make himself like the most high God.

The Bible describes, in the book of Isaiah, chapter fourteen and verses twelve to fifteen, how Satan fell from heaven, the one who was called Lucifer and the son of the morning. So he had position in heaven until he said in his heart that he will exalt his throne above the stars of God and sit upon the mountain of the congregation and make himself like God.

With that thought, he broke heavenly protocol and so was cast down from heaven. The book of Ezekiel chapter twenty eight also mentions how Satan was the anointed cherub that was set upon the holy mountain of God and used to walk up and down the midst of the stones of fire and how he was perfect from the day he was created until iniquity was found in him and he was cast out from heaven to earth. The book of revelation, chapter twelve, also describes how there was war in heaven and Satan and his angels fought against the angel Michael and the angels of God but Satan was defeated and was cast down from heaven to earth and he still works to deceive the world.

Satan or Lucifer or the anti-Christ has tried to be equal with God since time immemorial and it will continue to be like that until Jesus come because deceiving the world is his form of revenging God and that is why he will do everything opposite God. Let me refer to the garden of Eden one more time. Genesis 3:1–5 (KJV) says, "Now the serpent was more subtle than any beast of the field which the LORD God had made. And he said unto the woman, Yea, hath God said, Ye shall not eat of every tree of the garden? And the woman said unto the serpent, We may eat of the fruit of the trees of the garden: But of the fruit of the tree which is in the midst of the garden, God hath said, Ye shall not eat of it, neither shall ye touch it, lest ye die. And the serpent said unto the woman, Ye shall not surely die: For God doth know that in the day ye eat thereof, then your eyes shall be opened, and ye shall be as gods, knowing good and evil."

In this contest, the Lord God did not mean death as a physical death. He meant a spiritual death or a spiritual disconnection from Him. But when the serpent spoke to Eve, he made the word of God that He spoke to Adam and Eve sound like a physical death. So, when Eve realized she would not physically die after all, she gave in to Satan's lies. That is how Satan has operated since he was banished from heaven. He would twist the Word of God and misinterpret its meaning and present it to the world to accept. Again another scripture in the book of John, chapter ten and verse ten, which says that the thief who is Satan, has come to steal and to kill and to destroy but Jesus has come that we might have life in abundance.

He deceives you so you will not have an abundant life. So, whatever will steal your knowledge, joy, and peace, whatever will make people foolish and unwise and without common sense, if people will drug themself to death, if they will drink themself to be useless and unworthy, that is what Satan does so that mankind will deliberately go against the law of God.

You see, the Good News of God tells us how God makes us right in his sight. This is accomplished from start to finish by faith. As the scriptures say, "It is through faith that a righteous person has life. But God shows his anger from heaven against all sinful, wicked people who suppress the truth by their wickedness." They know the truth about God because he has made it obvious to all mankind through His moral likeness and spiritual personality in all mankind since creation. For ever since the world was created, people have seen the earth and sky. Through everything God made, they can clearly see His invisible qualities—His eternal power and divine nature. So really, mankind has no excuse for not knowing God.

Yes, they knew God, but they would not worship Him as God or even give Him thanks. And they begin to think up foolish ideas of what God is like. As a result, people's minds became dark and confused. Claiming to be wise, they instead became utter fools. And instead of worshiping the glorious, ever-living God, people worship idols made to look like mere people and birds and animals and reptiles.

So God, in His anger at the sin of the people, abandoned them to do whatever shameful things their hearts desired. As a result, they do vile and degrading things with each other's bodies. They trade the truth about God for a lie. So they worship and serve the things God created instead of the Creator Himself, who is worthy of eternal praise! Amen. That is why God abandoned them to their shameful desires.

Even the women turned against the natural way to have sex and instead, indulged in sex with each other. And the men, instead of having normal sexual relations with women, burned with lust for each other. Men did shameful things with other men, and because of this sin, they suffered within themselves the penalty they deserved, which is foolish thinking. Since they thought it foolish to acknowledge God, he abandoned them to their foolish thinking and let them do things that should never be done. Their lives became full of every kind of wickedness, sin, greed, hate, envy, murder, quarreling, deception, malicious behavior, and gossip. They are backstabbers, haters of God, insolent, proud, and boastful. They invent new ways of sinning, and they disobey their parents. They refuse to understand, break their promises, are heartless, and have no mercy. They know very well God's justice requires that those who do these things deserve to die, yet they do them anyway. Worse yet, they encourage others to do them, too.

The love of God for mankind is continuously demonstrated by the fact that God gave mankind our own free will and never compels anyone to make a choice but it is His will that mankind chooses to do right in the sight of God. However choices have consequences. If, by man's freewill, one chooses to be in same-sex union, I personally believe that the consequence is that there must be no children in such an environment in the first place as the whole arrangement is divinely unacceptable by God.

Adopting a child into such a union therefore will jeopardize their entire life. The question is why should an innocent child be adopted into such a divinely unacceptable environment to be exposed either knowingly or unknowingly to somethings that may have a strong influence on them in their life choices and decisions.

According to an article I came across on the internet, Pope Francis is revising the Ten Commandments, which was given to Moses by God as a covenant between God and His people. This is mentioned in the book of Exodus, in the twentieth chapter. God said to the His people, "I am the Lord your God, who rescued you from the land of Egypt, the place of your slavery, you must not have any other god but me. You must not make for yourself an idol of any kind or an image of anything in the heavens or on the earth or in the sea. You must not bow down to them or worship them, for I, the Lord your God, am a jealous God who will not tolerate your affection for any other gods. I lay the sins of the parents upon their children; the entire family is affected—even children in the third and fourth generations of those who reject me. But I lavish unfailing love for a thousand generations on those who love me and obey my commands. You must not misuse the name of the Lord your God. The Lord will not let you go unpunished if you misuse his name. Remember to observe the Sabbath day by keeping it holy. You have six days each week for your ordinary work, but the seventh day is a Sabbath day of rest dedicated to the Lord your God. On that day no one in your household may do any work. This includes you, your sons and daughters, your male and female servants, your livestock, and any foreigners living among you. For in six days the Lord made the heavens, the earth, the sea, and everything in them; but on the seventh day he rested. That is why the Lord blessed the Sabbath day and set it apart as holy. Honor your father and mother. Then you will live a long, full life in the land the Lord your God is giving you. You must not murder. You must not commit adultery. You must not steal. You must not testify falsely against your neighbor. You must not covet your neighbor's house. You must not covet your neighbor's wife, male or female servant, ox or donkey, or anything else that belongs to your neighbor."

In the article the Pope Francis said God has instructed Him to revise the Ten Commandments. How odd? Why will God go against His own word? The Pope was delivering mass in Spanish and spoke about importance of family in modern society saying, "It needs to be helped and strengthened, lest proper sense of the services which society as a whole provides." He went on to talk about how Christians are faced with ever-increasing temptations brought on by the evils of modern society. The Pope said the updated Commandments will reflect the changing times and include some minor rewording of the existing rules as well as the addition of two new Commandments. The Fourth Commandment, which advocates that proper respect be shown towards one's parents, has been reworded in order to include children raised by same-sex parents. Pope Francis said the Seventh Commandment, prohibiting adultery and, among other things, homosexuality, has been removed entirely, as instructed by God, in order to extend "God's grace to all His children." Addressing the inclusion of the new Commandments, which bring the total number to eleven, Pope Francis praised the rapid growth of technology in the digital age but said, "progress comes at a price." The new Fifth Commandment, which replaces the prohibition of adultery, forbids all aspects of genetic engineering and bans the consumption of genetically modified foods. Please refer to the article in *WORLD NEWS from realnewsrightnow.com Pope Francis: God Has Instructed Me to Revise the Ten Commandments, published on JULY 6, 2015 by R. HOBBUS J.D.* for full story.

The Bible states explicitly in the book of Revelations, chapter twenty two and verses eighteen to nineteen a solemn declaration to everyone who hears the words of prophecy written in the Bible from Genesis to Revelation, that if anyone adds anything to what is written in the Bible, God will add to that person the plagues described in the Bible. And if anyone removes any of the words from the Bible which is the book of prophecy, God will remove that person's share in the tree of life and in the holy city that are described in the Bible.

The Bible itself was written by men through divine inspiration which mean God inspired men by the power of the Holy Spirit to write His Word and for that matter, if God says not one word should be removed, added or changed from the Bible then absolutely no authority, power, influence, status, or government has the right to update the Bible whatsoever. This God-inspired word written by men is sanctioned by God, it is God-breathed and profitable for doctrine, reproof and correction which is instruction in righteousness and what is written is written.

We must turn to Jesus who said He is the bread of life and anyone that come to Him shall never hunger and he that believe in Him shall never thirst, to receive all the answers in order that we will be satisfied. Jesus has offered to lead mankind into all truth of the Word of God and so let us go to God through Jesus Christ to receive the sound understanding of His Word, by which to live and guard our path into righteousness continuously. That way mankind will be able to identify that which is the genuine true Word of God and that which is the false deception word of the anti-Christ. As the Bible says, in the book of Daniel chapter eleven and the verse thirty-two, that Satan will flatter and win over those who have violated the covenant but the people who know their God will be strong and will resist him.

Chapter 13

Godly Counsel

I believe the authority of the Word of God is invested into me as a humble servant of the most high God. He has filled me with His Holy Ghost and power and called me to exalt His name and to declare the acceptable year of our Lord. God has anointed me to preach of Jesus and of His crucifixion to carry the message of reconciliation and the repairing of the bridge between God and man.

I have thirty years of marriage but, with over thirty-five years of marriage counseling experience. I have also officiated and blessed more than twenty-five marriages. I am empowered and capable to give a sound and godly counsel on marriage which is a divine institution set up by God. Therefore I want to point out some factors to understand in this institution:

- Marriage is made up of a combination of two different people with different opinions, perspectives, analogies, skills, backgrounds, and characters
- The two must aim to make their union succeed

- The one who established the institution, God, must be the center of the marriage for it to be successful
- Marriage is an institution for learning, and where knowledge is acquired and applied into one's life to become better and wiser
- In marriage, we must remember that our spouse is subject to changes and when they change, we must learn to complement the change
- As the marriage grows, couples can be close in the physical yet so far and disconnected in thoughts plans and viewpoint and that only patience, communication and forbearance can reconnect them

A deliberate effort must be made by married couples to know each other so that they are not quick to blame judge condemn each other. God's divine power has granted to mankind everything pertaining to life and godliness, through the true knowledge of Him who called us by His own glory and excellence. And this divine power transcends all human capabilities. And so we can do all things through Christ Jesus who enables and strengthens us by this power which He has bestow upon us. Therefore let us endeavor to bring this divine power into the marriage so that the excellence of God will be seen through love.

We must work hard also to present ourself to God and receive his approval as a good worker, one who does not need to be ashamed and who correctly explains the word of truth and applies it in the marriage. Daily devotions, praying together, studying the Word of God together, going to church together and supporting each other in any ministry work. When it comes to house chores, helping each other and sharing domestic responsibilities like cooking, cleaning, doing grocery and raising children. Always endeavor to do things together. There is an old saying, "together is beautiful."

As mentioned earlier, we have our free will to choose, but our choices have consequences. As you make choices in the marriage life, let them be choices that are productive, prosperous, healthy and that which leads to advancing your lives and the lives of those in your surroundings. Let your mindset be like that which Jesus said that only death should part you and your spouse in this marriage and then do what is takes to build the marriage in the unity of Christ Jesus.

The Bible says, in Proverbs 3:1−8 (KJV) that, "My son, forget not my law; but let thine heart keep my commandments: ² For length of days, and long life, and peace, shall they add to thee. Let not mercy and truth forsake thee: bind them about thy neck; write them upon the table of thine heart so shalt thou find favour and good understanding in the sight of God and man. Trust in the LORD with all thine heart and lean not unto thine own understanding. In all thy ways acknowledge him, and he shall direct thy paths. Be not wise in thine own eyes: fear the LORD AND depart from evil. It shall be health to thy navel, and marrow to thy bones."

When we keep the Word of God dear to our heart and pay attention to what He says, everything is alright .

Marriage situations that may seem so impossible to resolve just disappears at the mention of the name of Jesus. If you feel you have reached a dead end in the marriage and there is no way forward, give Jesus a chance and see how He will turn it all around for you and make it beautiful.

At this point, if you do not know Jesus, I want to invite you to give your life to Him accepting Him as your Lord and personal savior, if you have not already done so. You see, for you to understand the marriage institution, you need to have Jesus in your heart. His Word must dwell in you for you to activate His divine power to show His excellence and glory in your life. Marriage is all about God and the great plans He has for you. And so Jesus is the only one who can help you through your marriage. John 1:12 (KJV) states, "But as many as received Him, to them gave He power to become the sons of God, even to them that believe on His name."

You are empowered and given the right to enjoy the privilege of your sonship when you become a child of God by accepting Jesus. And when you are empowered then you are a new creation, transformed spiritually reborn by Jesus Christ and made a new creature. This means that the old you, the natural carnal man which was sinful unforgiving shellfish, is gone and a new you begin. A new life in Christ Jesus, as the Bible describes who you have become, look into 1 Peter 2:10, that once you were not a people at all but now you are God's people, once you had not received mercy but now you have received mercy. This is the privilege of your sonship that you obtain mercy and be able also to show mercy to others, doing good caring and thinking of others in a positive way.

I would like to make it easy for you for you to be able to accept Jesus as your Lord and Saviour and so I have included a simple prayer for you to pray and believe.

A Prayer for Salvation

> Lord Jesus, I thank you that I have read Your Word in this book and I have known that for God so loved the world that He gave us you, that whosoever believe in You should not perish but have everlasting life. With my mouth, I confess that be merciful to me a sinner for I am sorry for my sins, cleanse me in Your precious blood that You shed for me; and I invite You into my heart from today as I accept you my Lord and personal Savior. I thank you that I am a brand-new person. My old sinful ways are gone and the new me has come. I am no longer a slave to sin. I am a child of God. Lord, help me walk in your ways. In Jesus' name, amen.

If you do not already have one, you will need to get a Bible and a simple Bible study plan to help you learn step by step practical Christian living into gradually growing your faith in Jesus Christ. And pray for God to lead you to find a local word-based church where you can become

part of. If you need assistance in any of these please con-
tact the International Prayer Palace Church at www.prayer-
palace.com.

To Our Readers,

We are thankful to God for your life, the fact that you took time to read *The Marriage Institution*. I hope that if you are married, your marriage will be enriched with the blessings of God. If you are single, I hope you have been blessed with divine guidance and that by God's help you will find the right better half. I pray for you that the God of peace who brought up from the dead our Lord Jesus, the Great Shepherd of the sheep, through the blood that sealed and ratified the eternal covenant, equip you with every good thing to carry out His will and strengthen you, accomplishing in you that which is pleasing in His sight, through Jesus Christ, to whom be the glory forever and ever. Amen.

Acknowledgments

My acknowledgment goes to all International Prayer Palace Church saints, past and present, who have formed a vital part in my walk with God, my spiritual growth, my experience and knowledge acquired into writing this book. I acknowledge them exclusively because, without these numerous wonderful saints who now form part of my life, I would not have had a ministry.

I acknowledge and give God the glory for the Overseer and presiding Bishop of the International Prayer Palace Church, Apostle Samuel Y. Agyei.

I acknowledge the honorable Bishop Darrell Jake Jacob and First Lady Cheryl, who have shown uncommon selfless love to my husband, myself, and our family.

I acknowledge all my ministry partners and friends and the network of pastors, who have encouraged, comforted, and supported me in ministry.

I acknowledge my niece, Vanessa Badmos, and her husband, Sheyi Badmos, who allowed themselves to hear from God concerning publishing this book.

I acknowledge all who will take the time to read this book. I pray that the God who gives perseverance and encouragement grant them the ability to be of the same mind with one another according to the plans and purposes that Christ Jesus has for them, so that with one accord, they will glorify the God and Father of our Lord Jesus Christ. Amen

Finally, I acknowledge the entire International Prayer Palace Church (IPPC). I owe my spiritual growth to them. I thank God for the countless opportunities through IPPC to teach, preach, counsel, dedicate children, officiate marriages, and more. I also thank God for the national and international recognition I have gained as a motivational, inspirational speaker of the sound, unadulterated, genuine Word of God.

References.

1. Information on Domestic Abuse Statistics | lwa.org.uk
    www.lwa.org.uk/understanding-abuse/statistics.htm

2. Information on Pope Francis, source – WORLD
    NEWS from realnewsrightnow.com Pope Francis: God
    Has Instructed Me to Revise the Ten Commandments,
    published on JULY 6, 2015 by R. HOBBUS J.D.

Information 1- on 10 Wedding Traditions from Around
    the World By Stephanie Pappas November 01, 2011
    on livescience.com

Information 2–on Western European wedding, source–
    copyright 2002-2004 Euroevents & Travel, LLC online

Information 3–on world marriage traditions, source–
    ivillage.ca

Scriptures are taken from the AMPLIFIED
    VERSION (AMP)

KING JAMES VERSION (KJV)

NEW AMERICAN STANDARD BIBLE (NASB)

NEW LIVING TRANSLATION (NLT)

Biography

*P*astor Joyce Nyante was born to parents who were members of the Presbyterian Church, and therefore, she was raised as a Presbyterian. She accepted the Lord Jesus as her Savior and became born again in 1977, then she left the Presbyterian church and joined the Assemblies of God Church, which was a Pentecostal church. Pastor Joyce also partnered with the Powerhouse Evangelistic and Prayer Group while in the Assemblies of God church. Later, a group from the Powerhouse branched out to plant the Miracle life Christian Centre in 1984; she was part of that group. While attending the Assemblies of God church, Pastor Joyce joined DULOS, an American evangelistic ship that has sailed to multiple countries to spread God's word. She later got married in 1990, acquired a university degree in Accounting and Finance and further attained Theology and biblical Studies qualification in a bible college. She has since become a preacher, teacher, evangelist, and a pastor, doing God's work internationally.

Academic Achievements

+ Evangelist training and discipleship at Morris Cerullo School Of Ministry England

- BA(HONS) accounting and finance at Thames Valley University, England
- Theology and biblical studies at International Prayer Palace Church Bible Institute, Ghana
- Ordained evangelist, pastor, and teacher

CPSIA information can be obtained
at www.ICGtesting.com
Printed in the USA
LVHW070000280321
682703LV00022B/1621